About this book

This is the third in a series covering the London Livery Companies, London's Inns of Court, its Pall Mall Clubs, and (eventually) the Royal Societies and Institutions. What all these interesting entities have in common is the fact that they are a peculiarly English way of doing things, of meeting a socio-economic need, of performing a role within the contemporary world – the Livery Companies surviving from their origins in the middle ages and the Inns also as relics from the medieval period, but both continuing to fulfil important modern purposes; while the Clubs are a unique concentration of similar organisations (some dating back more than 250 years) unknown in such density anywhere else on the planet, and the Royal Societies and Institutions are an equally extensive and special way of organising and recognising intellectual, academic, and scientific activity. At the back of this book there are brief notes on the two other books so far published within this projected quirky quartet.

Of what we shall refer to as 'Our Clubs' suffice to say for this blurb that they are in good financial shape in the second decade of their third century of existence as an organisational form, albeit that there have been closures and mergers during the 1960s to the 1980s which have reduced the total number from a peak in the Edwardian era. The concept of 'Clubland' (centred on Pall Mall and St James's Street, stretching onto Piccadilly) remains intact and the English continue to congregate within these magnificent 'Clubhouses'. We will explore these Clubs - their history and their organisation, their legal status, and how they are viewed in literature and on film. We will consider the mythology attaching to them, and ask whether at least some of them were (perhaps still are) the lair of 'The Establishment'. Why were English gentlemen in Victorian and Edwardian times so very 'clubbable', creating the concept of 'the gentlemen's club' and founding so many of them as an evolution from their eighteenth-century rather more rakish precursors that had in turn emerged from the coffee-houses and the taverns serving as Restoration meeting places which were the focus of the new concept of the expression of 'public opinion' and of activity within 'the public sphere'?

What has been written about 'Our Clubs' over the decades? – with luck EVERYTHING ever published about them is (the author ambitiously hopes!) collected in the Bibliography, and, as far as I can see, there has been no comprehensive contemplation of 'Our Clubs' for over a century. Do the Clubs continue to have 'dress-codes'? – yes, indeed they do! And do applicants for membership still get 'black-balled'? – they are, albeit only on rare occasions. Are members ever expelled? – seemingly and very occasionally, yes (usually - and quite rightly - for being obnoxious to Club staff). Has the cuisine of Clubland moved beyond roast beef and spotted dick, washed down by lashings of claret and custard? – without doubt. What image do they seek to project for 2020? – and, regardless, how does the media view them? What is said about them in cyberspace? Will they survive collectively or will their ranks be thinned over coming decades? Will certain (a very few) of them never admit women to membership? Is being 'clubbable' compatible with the age of the mobile-phone and the urge to 'tweet'? Are they threatened by the recent wave of trendy proprietor-clubs (pioneered by Soho House) now spreading across London and indeed well beyond, themselves an echo of the eighteenth-century proprietor-clubs that pre-dated Our Clubs? This little book, then, is a discussion of 'clubbery' for the 'clubocracy' of 'clubical' folk.

A compendium of images taken from old books on Our Clubs is slotted in after the Index, simply for browsing through at leisure.

LONDON'S PALL MALL CLUBS

David Palfreyman

From O'Connor, A. (1976)

Palfreyman's London series:

London's Livery Companies (2010, hardback, 390pp)

London's Inns of Court (2011, hardback, 370pp)

London's Pall Mall Clubs (2019, paperback)

London's Royal Societies, Institutions, and Colleges (forthcoming)

'Clubs' is available from Amazon in both a paperback (£10) and a Kindle format (£5). The 'Livery Companies' and the 'Inns' hardback books can also each be obtained for £10 each (plus £2.50 for P&P) direct from the author at New College, Oxford, OX1 3BN (cheque made payable, please, to 'David Palfreyman').

London's Pall Mall Clubs

Man is said to be a Sociable Animal, and, as an Instance of it, we may observe, that we take all Occasions and Pretences of forming ourselves into those little Nocturnal Assemblies, which are commonly known by the name of 'Clubs'. (Addison, 'The Spectator', 10 March 1711)

David Palfreyman, OBE FRSA MA MBA LLB

Bursar & Fellow, New College, University of Oxford

Director, Oxford Centre for Higher Education Policy Studies

Freeman Member of the Worshipful Company of Educators

Member of the Oxford & Cambridge Club

First published in Great Britain 2019 by David Palfreyman through Kindle Direct Publishing and the Independent Publishing Network.

The right of David Palfreyman to be identified as author of this work has been asserted by him in accordance with the Copyright, Designs and Patents Act 1988.

© David Palfreyman

ISBN 978-1-09470-615-3

British Library Cataloguing in Publication Data.
A record for this book can be obtained from the British Library.

All rights reserved; no part of this publication may be reproduced, stored in a retrieval system, or transmitted in any form of by any means, electronic, mechanical, photocopying, recording, or otherwise without either the prior written permission of the Publisher or a licence permitting restricted copying in the United Kingdom issued by the Copyright Licensing Agency Ltd, 90 Tottenham Court Road, London, W1T 4LP. This book may not be lent, resold, hired out or otherwise disposed of by way of trade in any form of binding or cover other than that in which it is published, without the prior consent of the Publisher.

Also by David Palfreyman:

- 'The Law of Higher Education' (Oxford University Press, with Dennis Farrington)
- 'Reshaping the University – The Rise of the Regulated Market in Higher Education' (Oxford University Press, with Ted Tapper)
- 'Universities and Colleges – A Very Short Introduction' (Open University Press, with Paul Temple)
- 'The Oxford Tutorial' (OxCHEPS – Chinese edition from Peking University Press)

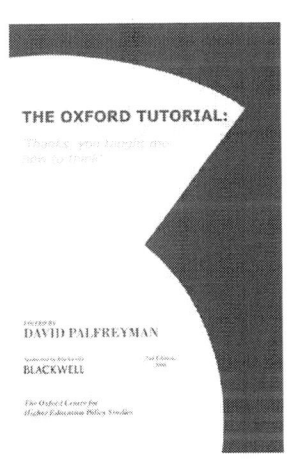

Contents

Preface	1
Introduction	7
Chapter I – The Club in History	22
Chapter II – The Club in Literature	59
Chapter III – The Club in Law	81
Chapter IV – The Club in Practice	100
Conclusion – The Clubs in Future?	116
Appendices: List of Clubs Past, Present, New, and Fictional	128
Bibliography	144
Index	156
A Compendium of Images	159
A brief note on the two sister volumes	164

Preface

Pall Mall, a street of palaces, mostly clubs.

Hatton, 'Clubland: London and Provincial', 1890

In Pall Mall there were… some rustic sightseers draining the last dregs of daylight in an effort to make out from their guidebooks which of these reverend piles was which…

Childers, 'The Riddle of the Sands', 1903

This book is the third in a Series looking at four sets of quaint and quirky, quintessentially English institutions the likes of which on such a scale or indeed at all exist globally only within London: the Livery Companies, the Inns of Court, the Pall Mall Clubs, and the Royal Societies. My interest in them stems from having read History at Oxford (Queen's, 1972-75) and spending the past thirty years as the Bursar of and a Fellow of another of Oxford's oldest colleges (New College, Founded 1379): were the Oxford – and Cambridge – colleges actually in London they would be the obvious subject of a volume five in the Series as also being oddly English, and like the Livery Companies and the Inns long-lasting adaptable medieval creations (I have in fact published a little book on the unique Oxford Tutorial as the colleges' quaint and quirky means of teaching undergraduates).

I accept that this volume might just as readily have been entitled 'The Clubs of St James's, London' since, of course, not all the Clubs here discussed are on Pall Mall, but that title seemed clumsy and spoilt the idea of London's this and that ('London's Livery Companies', 'London's Inns of Court'); while a title of 'London's Clubs' or 'London's Clubland' might have raised hopes of interesting content that would have been sadly dashed – even if sales might have been lucratively enhanced!

So, let's settle for 'London's Pall Mall Clubs' – recognising the geography of Clubland from the comments of an American observer (Alfred Kinnear in 'Munsey's Magazine') who back in 1902 noted: 'Present day Clubland extends in a zig-zag course from the bottom of Waterloo Place along Pall Mall, up St James's Street, to the middle of Piccadilly'. And also acknowledging his comment that 'the real centre of Clubland is Pall Mall' - 'Pall Mall, the Street of Clubs' and 'Here stand the greatest clubs known to Englishmen'. Moreover, after all, it is possible to buy on Amazon, for a very modest price, a splendid 'vintage metal sign' carrying the legend in red and black on white: * Gentlemen's Clubs * PALL MALL * SW1 * LONDON * (as reproduced on the back-cover of this book).

As with the first two volumes here I follow much the same format - and, as also with those books, I make no claim that here there is profound original research - other than, as when 'researching' the Livery Companies, I have been rigorous in dining in as many Clubs as I did in Company Halls, such is my commitment to scholarly endeavours. The standard approach has been applied: the history of the Clubs (beginning with the Restoration coffee-houses rather than needing to go back to the first Livery Company as the Weavers from 1155 or to the early days of the Inns dating from over a century later) ; their depiction in literature (and on TV and film); what they are as legal entities and businesses; their customs and practices, assets and treasures, finances and accounts, committees and officers; and a conclusion considering their survival into this new century. As usual an attempt is made to provide a comprehensive Bibliography before

Preface

so many works just get forgotten (the London Library has an extensive collection of books on the Clubs and Clubland, taking up a couple of shelves in its wonderfully accessible stacks). Again, as with the earlier volumes, I have inserted images from the old texts – masses of modern photographs of the various existing Clubs can be found at their websites and at Google Images, so here it is more interesting to see long-lost images from the past, which for this book I have assembled together in a Compendium rather than mingled in amidst the text; browse the Compendium of Images as your leisure!

Might 'Our Clubs', as indeed for any of these London institutions eventually become utterly unfashionable and absurdly anachronistic? Could these entities be ruthlessly superseded in the way Trollope's odious Mr Slope, the Bishop's Chaplain, scares gentle Precentor Harding (in Chapter XIII, 'The Rubbish Cart', of *Barchester Towers*, 1857): 'New men are carrying out new measures, and carting away the useless rubbish of past centuries!'. Trollope comments: 'A man is sufficiently condemned if it can only be shown that either in politics or religion he does not belong to some new school established within the last score of years. He may then regard himself as rubbish and expect to be carted away... This new doctrine of Mr Slope and the rubbish cart...'.

Or will these Clubs survive, avoiding Mr Slope's rubbish cart (as, say, the Livery Companies narrowly escaped abolition by the Royal Commission of the 1880s - or indeed as the Oxford colleges still potter on in an age of higher education bureaucracy, metrics, and standardisation) by continuing to adapt to their times (female members and now wi-fi in the Clubhouse!)? Will they always be there to fulfil the role that Trollope described in his *An Autobiography* (Chapter IX, 1883): 'In 1861 I became a member of the Garrick Club... Having up to that time lived but very little among men, having known hitherto nothing of clubs, having even as a boy been banished from social gatherings, I enjoyed infinitely at first the gaiety of the Garrick… The Garrick Club was the first assemblage of men at which I felt myself to be popular. I soon became a member of other clubs… the Arts Club… the Civil Service Club… the Athenaeum… the Cosmopolitan… the Turf…'.

That said, even if clubbery and the clubocracy flourish, might the centre of gravity for modern clubbable folk in the new millennium be shifting to the trendy tieless proprietor clubs created over the past couple of decades? - a process started by Nick Jones in founding Soho House (which is now a global network located in most 'world cities': and even with a retreat from the furious pace of city life on offer in the depths of the English countryside at Great Tew in the form of the aptly named Soho Farmhouse).

In writing the book on the Livery Companies I discovered that the previous attempt at a comprehensive study had been undertaken by Colonel Blackham in 1931. When embarking on the Inns of Court project I was astonished (indeed, even spooked!) to find again that Colonel Blackham had tackled the same topic in 1932. It would have indeed been bizarre if the energetic Colonel had taken on the Clubs in 1933, but the only previous wide-ranging studies of the Clubs are from more than a century ago: Griffiths, 1907, *Clubs and Clubmen* ; Nevill, 1911, *London Clubs* ; and Escott, 1914, *Club Makers and Club Members*. These three works will, of course, be much cited later in the text – along with a few from earlier decades: Hatton, 1890, *Clubland* ; Ivey, 1880, *Clubs of the World* ; Timbs, 1866, *Club Life of London* ; and Marsh, 1828, *The Clubs of London*. I have little doubt, however, that the dear Colonel Blackham was a member of one or more Clubs, given that he was a Liveryman of three Companies (and Clerk of one) as well as a member of two Inns. In fact, the book closest to the format of this 2018 offering is the 1907 one by Major Griffiths, but I fear the present humble author did not even do National Service let alone reach the rank of Major (nor still less Colonel as for Blackham).

The most recent book on our Clubs has, of course, been the splendid *The Gentlemen's Clubs of London* (Anthony Lejeune, 2012, as an updated version of earlier editions dating back to 1979): this modest text in no way seeks to compete with that lavishly illustrated volume. There is a 1964 book by Girtin (*The Abominable Clubman*) which investigates 'the anatomy of Clubs' in a 'goodhumoured' way - and between Griffiths et al in the Edwardian era and Lejeune's various editions during the 1970s and 1980s this 1964 text seems to have been the only fairly wide-ranging exploration of our Clubs as a social and organisational phenomenon (Darwin's *British Clubs* from 1943 is a very short study). Otherwise there have been recent and important scholarly studies of particular aspects of clubs: Black (2012) offers 'a literary-cultural study of Victorian Clubland'; Clark (2000) gives us the social history of clubs (1580-1800) as very widely defined; Doughan & Gordon (2006) focus on women and clubs; and Milne-Smith (2011) provides 'a cultural history of gender and class in Late Victorian Clubland'.

The manuscript has benefited greatly by being read in its entirety by my good friends Geoffrey Bennett and Jonathan Edmunds, and also from conversation over the Club Table with another, (sadly now the late) Brian Iverson: to all of whom I am deeply indebted - its remaining errors or omissions are hence entirely due to my own incompetence. Thanks are also owed to the Librarian of the Oxford and Cambridge Club for his expertise and enthusiasm in helping locate material for this volume, as indeed for the two others in the Series. And a very great debt indeed is owed to Harry Browning, who rescued the manuscript that had been lurking in Word format for rather a long times since I lacked the patience and courage to tackle the software so as to covert the text for Kindle uploading and then for lodging at the Amazon website as a print-on-demand-paperback: Harry dealt calmly and magnificently with all that. Finally, as a Member of the Oxford and Cambridge (and indeed, if I may, on behalf of all the many members of all the many Pall Mall and St James's Clubs) appreciation and gratitude are due to the legions of hard-working and expert staff that make these places function as oases of civilisation - as Girtin (1964, p 199) comments: '… the whole existence of the club was, and is, utterly dependent upon the quality of its staff'.

This book is dedicated to the memory of Brian Iverson, stalwart member of the Oxford & Cambridge Club and an Old Member of New College, Oxford.

David Palfreyman,

The Library of the Oxford & Cambridge Club,

New Year 2019

Introduction

If the ancient Lacedemonians invented clubs, the modern English may take the credit of having perfected them.

Hatton, 'Clubland: London and Provincial', 1890

Of the making of clubs there is no end.

Griffiths, 'Clubs and Clubmen', 1907

The object throughout has been… to trace and illustrate the connection of the club system generally… with the social, political, intellectual, and moral tendencies or characteristics of the period during which they grow up… The evolution of the club may be summed up in a sentence as the progress from a house of call to a centre of interest, a school of character, and a social training-ground.

Escott, 'Club Makers and Club Members', 1914

The *OED* defines 'Club' (leaving aside 'club' as 'a disease in cabbages or turnips') as: 'A meeting or assembly at a tavern etc for social intercourse' (probably based on Johnson's 1755 *Dictionary* and also Addison in 1711 noting 'those little Nocturnal Assemblies, which are commonly known by the name of Clubs'); and (for our prime purpose) 'An association of persons (admittance into which is usually guarded by ballot), formed mainly for social purposes, and having a building (or part of one) appropriate for the exclusive use of the members... may be political, literary, military, etc... but its main feature is to provide a place of resort, social catering, and entertainment'. The *OED* gives the earliest use of 'club' in the second sense, as explored in this book, from Walpole in 1776 referring to Almack's Club and then Byron in 1823 commenting on Watier's as the Dandy Club. The derivation of 'club' is from 'clubbe, clobbe' in Middle English, in turn from Old Norse 'klubba' as an assimilated form of 'klumba' which is related to 'clump' from 'klumpe' in Middle Low German.

The *OED* adds that: 'The institution has developed into its most completely-organised form in London, where, especially in the vicinity of St James's (colloquially called 'clubland') , are to be found the most perfect types of it' – Horace Walpole (1776) is cited: 'Being excluded from the unfashionable club of young men at Almack's they formed a plan for a new club. They built a magnificent house in St James's Street and furnished it gorgeously.'. Following on from 'club' used for Our Clubs and Clubland we get, inter alia: club-house, club-dinner, club-night, club-hour, club-armchair (G.B. Shaw, 1919: 'Fat old men, sitting comfortably in club chairs.'), club-fender, club-law, club-man, club-men, and (of course) club-bore. (The *OEDonline* added in 2000 'club kid' as 'chiefly US: 'a young person who attends or belongs to a club; spec. one who frequents night clubs...') We also find in the *OED* – clubbish (1530, clownish or boorish; later, by the middle of the nineteenth-century, 'disposed or addicted to clubs'), clubbism, clubby, clubical, clubster, and (sadly for some) clubless. Johnson (but not in his *Dictionary*) gave us 'clubbable' (1783) and also 'unclubbable' (perhaps 1764), and thence come clubbability and clubbableness; while clubbery covers this book as a discussion of club affairs collectively, as peopled by and hopefully of interest to the clubocracy (*Daily News*, 7/10/1882: 'The clubocracy congregate around St James's Square.'). The term 'clubbing' as used by today's young comes from Pepys *Diary* (in a 1660 entry for visiting an assembly or club in the earlier sense or definition above).

Within 'Collins Dictionary' the word 'club' is, variously, 'a group or association of people with common aims or interests' and 'the room, building, or facilities used by such a group' – the two 'in combination' being the 'clubhouse' as 'a building in which elected, fee-paying members go to meet, dine, read, etc.'. In contrast to Our Clubs and their 'elected' members there is another version of a club as 'a commercial establishment in which people can drink and dance; disco' – admission being determined by the proprietor or management (or the whim of the bouncers) and by payment, sometimes on an annual basis. In addition, 'clubland' is '(in Britain) the area of London around St James's, which contains most of the London clubs' – duly frequented by the species 'clubman' and 'clubwoman' as an individual 'who is an enthusiastic member of a club or clubs'.

The famous *Dictionary* compiled by Samuel Johnson and published in 1755 defined 'Club' as 'an assembly of good fellows' citing Dryden, and 'Clubroom' as 'the room in which a club or company assembles' citing Addison – on the *Dictionary* see Hitchings, 2005; and on the making of the *OED* see Winchester (2003) and Gilliver (2016), plus a 2017 feature film! The also famous 1911 edition of the *Encyclopaedia Britannica* under 'Club' discusses 'a term given to a particular association of persons', starting with Ancient Greece (where clubs were like the medieval guilds or livery companies with annually elected officers taking an oath on admission to office – Palfreyman, 2010) and then in Ancient Rome (again, often trade or craft guilds as collegia opificum; but later in addition as political associations, collegia sodalicia, which were often suppressed; and as cults (sodalitates) along with funeral and burial clubs, as similarly to be found in medieval London). The entry progresses to 'Modern Clubs' in the 'modern sense of an association to promote good-fellowship and social intercourse' (dating from the time of 'The Tatler' and of 'The Spectator' in the early decades of eighteenth-century England, but with isolated earlier examples given of John Aubrey writing in 1659: 'We now use the word clubbe for a sodality in a tavern.').

The *EB* article notes that Charles II in 1675 proclaimed that the coffee-houses should be 'put down and suppressed' since therein 'divers false, malitious and scandalous reports are devised and spread abroad to the Defamation of his Majesty's Government' – here we find the beginnings of the concept of public opinion, and seemingly the coffee-houses could not be counted on as being part of 'The Establishment' in the way Our Clubs were alleged to be in later centuries (as discussed below). This entry in the 1911 edition estimates there are 'now upwards of a hundred' clubs in London, and states that: 'Almost every interest, rank and profession has its club.' – including, for women, the Alexandra (1884), the Empress (1897), the Lyceum (1904), and the Ladies Army & Navy (1904); plus a few mixed clubs such as the Albemarle and the Sesame. It is further noted that these clubs are, since the 1902 Licensing Act, 'within the purview of the licensing system' as applied even to 'the most exalted Pall Mall club'! Some US clubs are listed since there 'club-life' has now 'grown to enormous proportions' and 'the number of excellent clubs is now legion, and their hospitality proverbial': the Hoboken Turtle Club (1797); and in New York alone, the Union (1836), the Century (1847), the Union League (1863), the University (1865), the Manhattan (1865), the Lotus (1870), the Knickerbocker (1871), and the Metropolitan (1891).

In 'Murray's Modern London, 1860: A Visitor's Guide' we are taken to 'our sixth architectural centre, not inaptly called the centre

Introduction

of social and political life. Here we are in the heart of Clubland. '. We are walked along Pall Mall from Waterloo-Place and then up St James's Street, past 'White's' and 'Boodle's' as 'once fashionable political Clubs, but now principally resorted to by elderly country gentlemen…'. We are advised that: 'The stranger should endeavour to procure orders (given by members) to see some of these Clubs [containing many 'very beautiful' rooms].' (pp xxi-xxii). The 'Principal Clubs in London' (26 of them) are tabulated and are detailed (pp 218-225) – along with the non-Club 'Steaks' as a collective of members dedicated to 'Beef and Liberty'. We learn, inter alia, that: 'The Army and Navy Club has 'a separate cook for chops, steaks, and kidneys'; the 'keep' of Club servants 'is said to be from 10s to 12s per week', but the 'Conservative Club House' ('owing to judicious management') got away with under 3s 8d (clearly no Minimum Wage there, still less a Living wage); the windows of the Reform are 'too small' and its water comes from a well that is 360 feet deep; the Athenaeum has a (then) new and trendy non-smoking room, 'a club-rarity in London'; the Union Club House has the largest wine stock; and the Whittington Club plus the Metropolitan Athenaeum on the Strand cater to 'the humbler classes'. Pall Mall is described as a 'spacious street' where Pepys' 'Diary' records him as going 'clubbing' in 1660 (pp 258/9). St James's Street like Pall Mall has a number of Clubs (pp 264/5).

A couple of years later in 'Bradshaw's Illustrated Hand Book to London' (1862) we are 'walked' to Pall Mall on the 'Fifth Day's Route.' – 'The Club-Houses, those most magnificent buildings where the most distinguished members of the worlds of fashion, politics, and literature meet for the purposes of lounging away their spare hours in conversation, reading, and refreshment, are now around us on every side… the lines of stately edifices that adorn this locality'. Then into St James's Street, which has 'some buildings worthy of notice' (White's, Boodle's, Brooks's, Arthur's). By 1888 we have

'Dickens's Dictionary of London: An Unconventional Handbook' (compiled by the son of Charles Dickens), in which many of Our Clubs have individual entries: the Athenaeum, for instance, 'possesses one of the best club houses, and the finest club library' (annual subscription, 'eight guineas'). There is a list of some 110 'principal London clubs' – including those 'for ladies and gentlemen', those that are 'ladies only', and those where 'ladies are admitted as visitors' (the remaining 100 or so are, of course, strictly gentlemen only). Under 'Pall Mall' as 'a street of palaces' we are informed that 'everything is classical'; and under 'St James's Street' we are told that 'the splendour of the Clubs of Pall Mall has eclipsed those of St James's Street' - and that newer clubs here 'have nothing to do with the quiet and the fogeydom of the old clubs'!

For a more recent listing of our Clubs Past and Present we refer to 'The London Encyclopaedia' (edited by Ben Weinreb et al, 2008 third edition, Macmillan) – and see at the end of this volume the Appendices as the Lists of Clubs Past, Present, New and Fictional. The Weinreb volume, in addition, contains a comprehensive listing of the many coffee-houses, dating from just before the Restoration and into the early decades of the nineteenth-century, as well as of famous inns/taverns - clubs of various sorts met in all these establishments. The earliest London coffee-house is listed as Bowman's, St Michael's Ally, Cornhill, from 1652 – followed by the Rainbow in Fleet Street, 1658. We are also informed that Pall Mall takes its name from a sort of croquet game and was laid out as a fashionable residential street in 1661; the freehold is almost all Crown land, except for No.79 given by Charles II in 1676 to Nell Gwynne – indeed, the Crown Estate recently paid £67m for 117, Jermyn Street; and it now owns around half of the St James's area, with assets valued at about £1b (and record London rents are being hit as at 2016 in the West End – for instance, £185 per square foot at 8, St James's Street compared to, say, a mere £100 or so even in the

Introduction

City's new iconic 'Cheesegrater' tower: all of selfish interest as New College redevelops its Fenchurch Street site held since 1386 into a 16-storey £250m office block!).

But back to Pall Mall, dating as noted from 1661: it became populated by posh shops and coffee-houses - for example, the Smyrna opened in 1702, with (supposedly) Beau Nash lurking in its window desperately waiting to be seen by passing Polite Society (he being Richard Nash, 1674-1762; Jesus College, Oxford, and the Inner Temple; 'derived an income from accepting extravagant wagers and gambling'; moved to Bath in 1705 and established the Assembly Rooms, becoming 'unquestioned autocrat of Bath' and indeed 'king of Bath' - the *DNB*). Pall Mall then became dominated by our Clubs, and they are now accompanied by various corporate HQs and a few private equity funds not lurking up in Mayfair – and also increasingly by fine arts galleries relocating from the ultra-high rents of Mayfair. Its Star and Garter eighteenth-century tavern was an upmarket inn mentioned by Smollett in 'Humphrey Clinker': various clubs met there, such as the Brothers' Club, the Thursday Club, the Nottinghamshire Club, and the Jockey Club. Our St James's Street dates from the time of Henry VIII, and was first named in around 1660; paved in 1662, it took off as an area for coffee/chocolate-houses and later clubs, and also for fancy shops (rather than fine houses as in Pall Mall) – some of which shops are, of course, still there (such as Berry Bros (1698), the wine merchant; and Locke & Co, hatters).

'The Man's Book: The Indispensable Guide for the Modern Man' (Thomas Fink, 2014, Weidenfeld & Nicolson) has an entry for 'London Clubs', making the point that here in this book we are exploring what used to be called 'gentlemen's clubs' (a term with a rather unsavoury meaning in the USA): 'Like the paradox of Schrodinger's cat, when a women observes a gentlemen's club it ceases to be one.'. Fink lists some 45 Clubs and quotes Sala: 'The English are the only clubbable people on the face of the earth.' – in the Oxford 'Dictionary of National Biography' George Augustus Sala (1828-1896) is a 'journalist' who 'found in ordinary club life all the recreation he required', being a member of several clubs and founding the Savage Club in 1857, which he hoped would be 'a club of merry fellows': the clubbable and clubby Sala was the essence of the clubman, of clubbability, of clubbableness.

Even 'The Rough Guide to London' (2014) for back-packing students has a box covering 'The Gentlemen's Clubs' of Pall Mall and St James's Street. It warns the young tourist peering in at the Clubhouse entrances that here are to be found 'the final bastions of the male chauvinism and public-school snobbery for which England is famous'. The 'Time Out London' 2014 edition tells us that 'Pall Mall is lined with members-only gentlemen's clubs (in the old-fashioned sense of the word)'. And for the German visitor 'Baedeker Reisefuhrer London' (2013) has an entry for St James's Street and Pall Mall as 'die Hauptachsen von 'London's Clubland'… die beruhmstesten Londoner Clubs…'.

There are very useful entries on Our Clubs and clubs in a wider sense in 'Wikipedia', carefully compiled and rigorously updated as the work of one or more anonymous individuals, whose material has been invaluable in preparing the Lists within the Appendices: the expertise, energy, and enthusiasm of the Wikipedia contributor(s) needs to be gratefully acknowledged. The Wiki entries (at January 2016) are for: 'Gentlemen's club' with links to 'List of gentlemen's clubs in London' and to individual entries for most of the clubs listed (real, fictional; existing, defunct; in London, elsewhere in England, beyond). The Wiki entry points out that the peak for creating new clubs was the later decades of the nineteenth-century, but most members were a member of only one establishment – the record is

Introduction

probably Earl Mountbatten belonging to nineteen in the 1960s! They provided a venue for relaxation, an escape, a home-from-home, a male refuge, a gossip-shop, a place for male banter. As the entry notes: 'Although traditional gentlemen's clubs are no longer as popular or influential as they originally were, many have seen a significant resurgence in popularity and status in recent years.'.

These clubs are to be found all over the globe, but nowhere, of course, in such density as in London's Clubland – examples elsewhere within the UK (see the list of 51, mainly in London, given in 'Whittaker's Almanack 2016' at pp 573/4) include: the New Club in Edinburgh, the Clifton Club in Bristol, the Athenaeum in Liverpool, the Ulster Club in Belfast, the Western Club in Glasgow, the New Club in Cheltenham, the Norfolk Club in Norwich, and the Northern Counties Club in Newcastle (the first dates back to 1787). And there used to be many more – for instance, the Union Club in Manchester from 1825 along with the Arts Club (1879), the Racquets Club in Liverpool (burnt down in the 1981 Toxteth riots), the Hampshire Club in Winchester, the Yorkshire Club in York. Hatton (1890) has chapters on the flourishing fifty or so 'provincial' clubs in Birmingham, Leeds, Liverpool, Manchester, Glasgow and Edinburgh, and Belfast; noting that these cities compared to 'the metropolis go to bed early' and hence 'luncheon is the great meal of the day in provincial clubland'. Friedrich Engels, the wealthy revolutionary theoretician collaborating with (and financially propping up) Karl Marx to concoct the 'Communist Manifesto' (1848), was a member of several clubs in Manchester (aka 'Cottonopolis') during the middle decades of the nineteenth-century (including the Albert Club, the Brazenose Club, and the Anstalt Club for Germans living in Manchester) – Hunt, 2009, pp 182 & 210-212. In eighteenth-century Edinburgh the 'Oyster Club' – aka 'Adam Smith's Club' – included among its illustrious members not only the great Adam Smith but also James Hutton the geologist and Joseph Black the chemist.

Beyond the UK there are, for instance, the Philadelphia Club, the Yale Club in New York, the Toronto Club, the Melbourne Club, the Durban Club, the Phoenix Club in Lima, the Royal Bachelors' Club in Gothenburg, the many clubs in India (the Bangalore Club, the Bengal Club in Kolkata, the Madras Club in Chennai, and so on). Most of these clubs world-wide operate a reciprocity network so that membership of, say, one's London Club gives access to others when travelling. On the history of the American clubs and their importing of the traditions of the London Clubs see chapter 2 of Kendall (2008); on, as an example, the history of the Harvard Club of New York see Kay (1995) – on the French nineteenth-century provincial gentlemen's bourgeois 'cercle' see Harrison (1999). The 1879 'Appleton's General Guide to the United States and Canada' lists Clubs in New York (Century, Knickerboker, Manhattan, Union, Union League, Lotus, Army & Navy), Philadelphia (Union League, Reform, Penn, Philadelphia, Social Art Club), Boston (Somerset, Union, Central), Chicago (Chicago, Union, Owl, Standard, Calumet), Cincinnati (Queen City, Phoenix, Allemania, Eureka, Cuvier), St Louis (Germania, University – and 'other club-houses of less note'), San Francisco (Union – its stone 'quarried and cut in China', Olympia, Bohemian, the San Francisco Verein), and New Orleans ('about twenty clubs', including Boston, Pickwick, Shakespeare, Jockey) – but, oddly, none are listed for 'Washington City'.

For Scruton (2006) the role of clubs features in his reviewing the essence of England, Englishness, and the English: the Englishman's love of joining things, filling 'their lives with local forms of membership', with 'focal points of local but durable loyalties' – 'Indeed, they related more easily to clubs, regiments, schools and teams than to human beings'; all as entities with 'the same 'clubbable' instinct, which prefers custom, formality and ritualised membership to the hullabaloo of crowds' (p 13/14). And popular even if another common characteristic is (or at least was) 'Nursery food': 'This flavourless stodge was the matter to which English eccentricity gave its many forms. And it was dutifully served up in all those institutions – public schools, Oxford and Cambridge colleges, gentlemen's clubs – which had the reproduction of Englishness as their tacit social goal.' (p 51). Thus, Our Clubs as 'the gentlemen's club' – (as Scruton sees it, pp 171/2) 'an institution created by the English in order to perpetuate the sense of belonging that they acquired in college and school' – promoted 'a code of decent behaviour, and where friendships were formal, dutiful and cold. Such was the gentlemen's club, and it was through the club that so many Englishmen refreshed their vision of community, exercised their sense of honour and formed those ties which sustained them in their working lives.'.

This Club, according to Scruton, was/is 'a corporate person, housed in a sacred precinct [Pall Mall, St James's] and known through its style. For the English gentleman it was not merely his true home, but also his moral and aesthetic tutor. The rich Turkey carpets, the mahogany and leather chairs, the regency dining tables, the walls lined with leather-bound books and musty portraits of forgotten worthies, the quiet smoking room, where old colonels slept behind their newspapers…' (pp 171/2). All supported by English Law and the flexibility of the law of trusts underpinning 'clubs, schools, colleges, universities, professional bodies, churches, the City Guilds, the Inns of Court' – a pervasive collection of legal entities: 'England was a society of corporate persons, objects of loyalty and duty which held people together while keeping them just sufficiently apart. English eccentricity flourished by virtue of the club, which protected the habits of its members, and reassured them that that their oddness would go unremarked.' (p 127) – for the legal status of the City Guilds and of the Inns see, respectively, Palfreyman 'London's Livery Companies' and 'London's Inns of Court' in this series; and for the concept of the membership contract and the trust for the ownership of Club assets see Chapter III of this book re 'The Clubs in Law'.

And all the minutiae of Club activity – as discussed in Chapter IV – are underpinned by the Club Rules and their application by its Management Committee; the Clubhouse is characterised by its various rooms with their restrictions re the use of mobiles or tablets/laptops; and Clubland is noted for selectivity in electing new members as well as problems in ending the membership of the club-bore. All features captured in this 1912 quote: 'Of the modern club two things may be said generally – first, it is necessary to form a committee to be cursed and reviled by all other members; and, secondly, it is desirable to have a library in which members may sleep and snore… [or even to be dead for a week within before being found, but at least such an] incident proves that a man is not interfered with in a well-regulated club if he is quiet and inoffensive… Old-fashioned gentlemen rather resent the introduction of the telephone into their clubs… The telephone in a club has the same effect on it that the Channel tunnel would have on Great Britain – the place ceases to be completely isolated… I was once on the committee of a club, and I know how earnestly the threatened resignation of some members is yearned for on many occasions. It is very difficult to find an opportunity of turning a member out of a club without laying the club open to the danger of an action in the law courts, and these growlers know that fact and trade on it.' (Hughes, 1912, Chapter 19, 'The English Clubmen').

There are many Club histories (new, recent, and old) which are occasionally referred to here in this book, but no attempt has been

Introduction

made to list them all - a random selection of recent ones popping up on Amazon would include, say: Lejeune (1993) on White's, Newark (2015) on the 'In and Out', Wansell (2004) on the Garrick, Hill (2009) on Boodle's, Thole (1992) on the Oxford and Cambridge, Ingamells et al (2013) and also Ziegler (1991) on Brooks's, Forrest (1968, 1979) on the Oriental, Dixon (2009) on the Army and Navy, Brendon (1997) on the RAC, Anderson (1993) on the Savile Club, Fulford (1962) on Boodle's, Jacoby (2000) on the East India, Fitzgerald (1968) on the Farmers Club, Petrie & Cooke (2007) on the Carlton, Hough (1986) on the Garrick, Cowell (1976) on the Athenaeum, Probert & Gilbert (2004) on the RAF Club, Perry (2003) on the Lansdowne, Woodbridge (1978) on the Reform. Most Clubs have informative websites, easily found via a few (careful) clicks on Google – these should be consulted for images of Clubhouses, external and internal; here in this book the images are reproduced from old books that might otherwise escape attention. The Google clicking needs, however, to be done with care lest the Reader accidentally happens upon various 'gentlemen's clubs' of a rather different kind from 'Our Clubs' but which have similar names and are located in less salubrious parts of London, in Texas, and elsewhere. Anthony Lejeune's various editions of his book on the Clubs (1979, 1984, 1997, 2012) gives us a wealth of fine photographs: as has been pointed out to me, the earlier books show the Clubs looking a little faded, sinking under the weight of falling memberships and increasing costs; while, happily, the 2012 new edition shows them positively glittering, if not sinking under the weight of gold-leaf unstintingly applied (much the same would apply to any photographic record of the Oxbridge colleges, except that dowdy dondom does not much favour gold-leaf…).

Anthony O'Connor captures neatly this 1960s/1970s era of the decline of the Clubs in his 'Clubland: The Wrong Side of the Right People' (1976). He himself 'for many years has been Secretary to a few great London clubs' whose various strengths and weaknesses are amalgamated into 'The Squires' Club' within this 'factional' account which notes that some clubs 'are falling by the economic wayside', not helped by the eccentric incompetence of their management: 'Club Secretaries were a special kind of breed, impoverished peers, retired colonels and paymaster commanders from the Royal Navy, who dispensed wisdom from an office chair… [and] hid somewhere in the huge mausoleums of Pall Mall' (the same syndrome applied to Domestic Bursars in Oxford colleges back then). He concludes with a parting shot at the equally dismal governance of the Clubs: 'One day I will retire from Clubland… [and I will not miss] the depressing atmosphere that is often fostered by indecision and lack of thought. Escalating costs are proving a nightmare for committees who meet, talk, and write reams of useless suggestions while their domain collapses around them.' . Of course, this was also the era of the decline of UK industry (think of British Leyland and the Austin Allegro or the Morris Marina!), whose management and governance suffered from much the same problems: but the Clubs were not propped up by taxpayer subsidies and hence some duly crumbled away faster than the British car industry, and nor did the Japanese version of Clubland move to fill the gap as eventually happened with Honda and Nissan in the 1980s, lured by regional development grants.

Instead the Clubs miraculously regained their financial strength sans Government aid and at the start of this new century, after some 250 years or so, London Clubland seems to be flourishing. Indeed, the demise – or at least the decline – of Clubland was also talked of in the 1900s, as Griffiths (1907) notes: 'We are told that London clubs are approaching the grand climacteric, that disease and decay are showing themselves, and that these time-honoured institutions, hitherto so full of vigorous growth, are verging upon decline.' (p 5). He then proceeds in the next 340 or so pages to refute this idea of

Introduction

'the alleged dry-rot' pervading London's Clubland, Clubs, and indeed also its Clubmen. In another comprehensive study of Clubland a few years later, however, Escott (1914) is rather less optimistic than Griffiths, seeing the desertion of the grand Victorian Clubhouse in favour of 'a return to the tavern clubs' and also viewing as a threat the emerging 'legion of first-class restaurants' (p 341): 'the twentieth-century club' has become expensive and dull, indeed very sober ('Costly wines for the most part enjoy the unbroken repose of the club cellar.' – p 342).

In this book we next explore in Chapter I the history of Our Clubs, and then turn in Chapter II to see how the Clubs have featured in fiction on the page and in film. Chapter III looks at the Clubs as legal and organisational entities, while Chapter IV considers their customs and eccentricities before we reach the Conclusion that contemplates the future of the Clubs. The Appendices provide listings of Clubs past, present, new, and fictional; and the Bibliography attempts to be comprehensive in recording every book ever written about Clubland (although not every single Club history) – a bottle of Oxford and Cambridge Vintage Club Claret is on offer to any Reader who alerts me to a significant work on the Clubs generally that has annoyingly escaped my toiling in the London Library, the Guildhall Library, the British Library, and the Bodleian Library…

Chapter I – The Club in History

Of all solemn bores, these Learned [Literary] Clubs are the most oppressive: they have little or no admixture of the natural and characteristic humours of men: the mind never sits there in its dishabille, but struts and marches in full-dressed coxcombry. So much talking, and so little said!

Marsh, 'The Clubs of London', 1828

Of all institutions, none have been more vitally and essentially English than Parliament and the club.

Escott, 'Club Makers and Club Members', 1914

We begin by rather randomly plucking history texts from my study shelves and searching the index for 'clubs' and their close relative 'coffee-houses'. Does Tombs, for example, in his splendid thousand page history of England find room for our clubs? Did the old nine volumes of the 'Pelican History of England' have space for them, or the almost complete nine volume replacement 'Penguin History of Britain'? What about the relevant volumes of the massive 'Oxford History of England' – and now more recently those in the emerging 'New Oxford History of England'? What can we glean about the history of clubs in English society and culture, and especially about the Pall Mall Clubs as, along with St James's Street and drifting up onto Piccadilly, London's Clubland?

Tombs (2014) has over twenty entries for 'clubs', beginning with 'Coffee House Culture' from the 1660s onwards as 'the public sphere' and 'the republic of letters' evolved – 'places and institutions for exchanging information and forming opinion' (p 293): the new coffee-houses, nationwide numerous debating societies covering philosophical as well as literary and scientific ideas, and such as the infamous 'Hellfire Club' for libertines and the 'Ugly Club' for the sadly less attractive. The arty 1734 'Society of Dilettanti' was dismissed by Hugh Walpole as one for which 'the nominal qualification… is having been in Italy, and the real one, being drunk' (p 297). In reviewing the anti-Establishment decade of the 1960s he notes that its institutions 'proved remarkably resilient and adaptive', including the fact that 'half a century on' we find 'gentlemen's clubs expanding' (p 791).

Moving on to the Penguin History of Britain series, Fleming (2010) comments that around 1,000 years ago wealthy folk 'were coming together to organise themselves into gilds centred on their local minsters' so as to ensure burial adjacent to their grand church, as in my own village of Bampton (Oxfordshire): these gilds were in effect 'dining and burial clubs' (p 331): 'low status dead' were consigned to a cemetery, albeit one still controlled by the Bampton minster church, some miles away in Chimney (p 332) – Bampton and its minster church are now, of course, globally famous as the village of 'Grantham' in 'Downton Abbey'. Kishlansky (1996) notes that the coffee-houses and the gentlemen's clubs emerged from the Restoration era and by the time of Queen Anne 'Whigs took their coffee and chocolate at St James's Coffee House and their whisky and wine at the Kit-Kat Club; Tories took theirs at the Cocoa Tree and the Society of Brothers' (p 318). In the related 'Pelican Social History of Britain' Porter (1982, p 245) asserts the very many (perhaps some 500) coffee-houses existing in London by 1700 were places for clergymen to write sermons, doctors to give consultations, and for political debate – in the case of one set up by Hogarth's father only in Latin! The clubs, notes Porter (p 172/3), were described by Addison as 'little nocturnal assemblies' and were created by all and sundry on all kinds of pretences – the Farters' Club, the Surly Club, the Sublime Society of Beefsteaks, the Lunar Society of Birmingham, the Lunatick Club of Essex; and gradually such clubs as White's and Almack's 'tolled the knell of coffee houses'. Similarly, the Royal Society (1660, and chartered 1662) effectively began earlier as an example of such 'nocturnal assemblies', as simply another dining society (Palfreyman, forthcoming).

From the first Oxford history series Clark (1956, p 358) sees the early coffee-houses as 'in fact clubs run for profit by their proprietors'; the word 'club' being then used for societies with fixed periodic meetings, and especially the literary clubs for 'the literary life of London was club-life' - 'It had the defects of club-life: there was more familiarity than intimacy; fashion counted for more than conviction; quickness in talk outshone depth of thought; it was worse to be laughed at than to be wrong. But club-life has its advantages. It brings out what men have in common; it helps them to set up common standards of judgement; it smooths away the idiosyncracies which hinder co-operation in common tasks.'. By the second half of the eighteenth-century London was 'honeycombed with clubs' of various kinds: 'The habitues of Almack's or Brooks's would, no doubt, be more excited by the turn of the card than a turn of phrase…' (Watson, 1960, pp 338/9). Plumb (1950) saw the myriad of clubs within eighteenth-century society (within London and beyond) in much the same way: '… some added to our cultural heritage… [others] were squalid breeding grounds of crime; the most socially valuable were the friendly (clubs and) societies… But they all made for quick interchange of opinion among men of the same class and tastes, for quick, active discussion of personalities and policies which touched their lives, and so helped to foster that sense of independence and decisive judgement which made England capable of democracy long before the reform of her oligarchic institutions.' (p 32 – the Great Reform Act that began the decades-long process of moving towards universal male and female voting did not appear until 1832).

Yet, difficult for Londoners even today to grasp, not all social and intellectual life was confined to London: indeed, the very first coffee-house opened in Oxford in 1650 (then London in 1652 - in St Michael's Alley, Cornhill) and Ipswich soon boasted eight; the Oxford Philosophical Society was founded in 1682; the Spalding Gentlemen's Society in 1710; the Stamford Society by 1721; and in 1715 Cambridge's Vice-Chancellor would designate only four tame publications allowed to be taken in the town's coffee-houses so that the undergraduates could 'have news without politics'. London, of course, offered the most venues for politics and distraction: an eighteenth-century student at one of the Inns mentions in his diary visiting twenty-four coffee-shops over eighteen months! And as a version of clubs there was an expansion of freemasonry: perhaps fifty or sixty lodges across the nation by 1725; again, as with the various clubs and the many coffee-houses, women were kept at bay as men met in these haunts - perhaps twenty-thousand a night went 'clubbing' in London alone according to a 1750 calculation. (Hoppit, 2000, pp 174/5, 182, 432-5; Langford, 1989, p 100.)

Our sort of clubs – the gentlemen's clubs of Pall Mall and across St James's – thus developed from this tradition of coffee-houses and literary or political clubs that emerged during the Restoration and thrived throughout the eighteenth-century. A few of Our Clubs date from these times but most, as was noted in the Introduction, are creations of the nineteenth-century, as will be discussed in detail below. Harrison (2009, 2010) in (for now, up to 1990) completing the 'New Oxford History of England' looks at the role of these Clubs in post-War Britain. He sees 1950s/60s 'upper-class fragmentation' (2009, p 197): 'Fragmentation within the elite is also reflected in the dwindling national importance of London's clubland. In the 1950s top people were already segregating themselves between clubs, with civil servants preferring the Reform, politicians the political clubs, financiers Brooks's, and so on. The clubs were now becoming less central to the elite social round. Whereas more than four-fifths of Edwardian MPs belonged to one or more London clubs, only two-thirds of Conservative and 8 per cent of Labour MPs belonged by 1974.' (Macmillan joined five and attended them regularly, but Eden avoided them – p 411; Jeremy Corbyn, Labour 'leader' at the time of writing is perhaps not a member of any…). Moreover, 'sex-segregated friendship' that had 'originated and flourished outside the home through the many semi-private enclaves within public life' (including 'fashionable London clubs') had been weakened by the 1960s as a means of mixing business and pleasure 'in an atmosphere of male companionship' (2010, p 284).

The two most famous politicians of the nineteenth-century displayed somewhat contrasting attitudes to 'clubbability' but similar ones in terms of not wanting always to be ultra-accessible to their MPs or others. Gladstone refused to join the Athenaeum lest he was badgered by its members, preferring instead the United University Club where seemingly he was ignored (not so at the Carlton where 'a group of tipsy Tories actually threatened him with physical violence when he was dining quietly alone' after he, as a Peelite, had savaged Disraeli's 1852 Budget: Blake, 1966, p 346). Disraeli in contrast (Blake, 1966, p 467) received a fine welcome at the Carlton after seeing off an attack by Gladstone on the 1867 Second Reform Bill, 'the enthusiastic members' imploring him to stay for supper – but he headed off home where his wife awaited him 'with a pie from Fortnum and Mason's and a bottle of champagne': his response to her being his famous words, 'Why, my dear, you are like a mistress than a wife.'. While Gladstone may not have found the Carlton at all congenial, he did enjoy, however, the select company at Grillions (elected 1840), a parliamentary dining club, and also at 'The Club' (elected 1857) as another dining society (Magnus, 1954, p 177 – who adds: 'The fact that Disraeli never belonged to 'The Club' may have possibly enhanced the attraction of its dinners.' – although see below…).

Disraeli was a later member of Grillions (elected 1865), and indeed eventually of 'The Club' (by 1868) as well as of the Athenaeum (1866) – the last having black-balled him in 1832. Bulwer Lytton suspected it was because Disraeli had 'written books people have talked about' as opposed to having 'compiled some obscure quarto which nobody had read' that would have made him 'sure of success'. Blake (1966, pp 434 & 449) notes that Our Clubs were a key part of Victorian politics in the age of Palmerston, Gladstone, and Disraeli, citing 'a contemporary journalist' who commented that Disraeli as Prime Minister relied on his Private Secretary, Monty Corry, for being kept informed about 'all the gossip of the clubs and all the chatter of the drawing-rooms'. And the gossip could be humorous, Blake repeating the 'jest' that 'went round the clubs' about the elderly Palmerston, as PM, having engaged in 'improper relations' with a Mrs Cain: 'she was certainly Cain, but was he Abel?'.

And certainly the young Disraeli 'tried to join a number of clubs, another crucial node of political life in early nineteenth-century London', but he 'was not yet deemed clubbable' (being rejected by the Travellers and the Athenaeum as 'a controversial figure'): Cesarani, 2016, p 51; as Blake (1966, p 271) comments: it was the era 'of the great political clubs, the Reform [the Whigs/Liberals] and the Carlton [the Conservatives], the effective headquarters of the two sides' (and also Cannadine (2017, p 165) on these two Clubs as the

HQs of new 'centralised party organisations' that were 'superseding the traditional aristocratic, political-cum-gambling clubs of White's (Tory) or Brooks's (Whig) [as now] too social, amateur and exclusive in the age of reform'). That said, when eventually admitted to Clubland (as part of 'the world of what would now be called 'the establishment'), 'Disraeli did not attend these societies more than courtesy required. He disliked men's dinner parties and went to them as a political necessity rather than a social pleasure.' (Blake, 1966, pp 81/2 and 435). Palmerston, however, was 'a man for clubs' (being a member of the Catch Club, of the Dilettanti Club, and of Almack's Club - although initially black-balled for 'The Club'): Guedalla (1926). In response to not being allowed to join 'The Club', Churchill and F.E. Smith promptly founded in 1910 'The Other Club' as a dining-society of 50 members of which no more than 24 could be MPs (Coote, 1971) – although Addison (2005, p 56) asserts that they created this new club in 1911 so that Liberals and Conservatives could be brought together after 'the bitterness caused by the House of Lords crisis' in 'a bipartisan dining club'.

Blake (1966, pp 505/505) expands on the mid-Victorian ruling class, elite, Establishment ('or whatever one wishes to call it') as being 'at least two distinct but overlapping circles': the traditional autocracy and squirearchy ('rich, grand, tolerant, often eccentric, not infrequently dissipated') who 'belonged to monosyllabic clubs' (White's, Boodle's, Buck's, Brooks's) - as opposed to 'the hard-working, serious-minded, gravely religious' rising middle-class professionals such as judges, divines, dons, and civil servants belonging to the Athenaeum, the Reform, the Oxford & Cambridge. Disraeli 'got along excellently' with the first group; being 'instinctively at home in the great houses' and appearing 'cool, sardonic, urbane'; while Gladstone displayed 'other-worldly indifference to the London dining-rooms' and retreated to the O&C – he belonged to the second group or division of the Establishment.

Yet, adds Blake (p759): 'There was something about Disraeli, which those who constitute that mysterious but nevertheless recognisable entity, 'the establishment', could never quite countenance…'.

Turning away from our several survey series of history texts, it is time to consider specific books which have material about clubs and also about the coffee-houses that flourished before them and then for a while alongside them. Macaulay in his famous 'History of England' (1848, Volume One, Chapter III on the state of England in 1685) considered the coffee-house to be 'a most important political institution' – the coffee-houses were 'the chief organs through which the public opinion of the metropolis vented itself': 'Every man of the upper or middle class went daily to his coffee house to learn the news and to discuss it. Every coffee house had one or more orators to whose eloquence the crowd listened with admiration, and who soon became, what the journalists of our own time have been called, a fourth Estate of the realm… Foreigners remarked that which especially distinguished London from all other cities; that the coffee house was the Londoner's home, and that those who wished to find a gentleman commonly asked, not whether he lived in Fleet Street or Chancery Lane, but whether he frequented the Grecian or the Rainbow… every rank and profession, and every shade of religious and political opinion, had its own head-quarters. There were houses near St James's Park where fops congregated… There were coffee houses where the first medical men might be consulted… There were Puritan coffee houses… and Popish coffee houses where, as good Protestants believed, Jesuits planned, over their cups, another great fire, and cast silver bullets to shoot the King…'. In Johnson's *Dictionary* (1755) there are more than thirty references to coffee and 'coffeehouse' is defined as 'a house of entertainment where coffee is sold, and the guests are supplied with newspapers' – Johnson meant 'conversation' when he used 'entertainment' (Hutchins, 2005, pp

151-153). On the history of the coffee-house see Cowan, 2005, and also Brewer, 1997.

Gatrell (2006) details the Georgian clubs of St James's – White's, Boodle's, Brooks's. There are reproductions of Rowlandson's depiction of 'The Brilliants', cavorting in their Covent Garden tavern club-room (p 89); of Hogarths's 'Midnight Modern Conversation' (p 290); of Cruickshank's 'Dinner at the Four in Hand Club at Salthill' (p 114), plus his 'Breaking Up of the Union Club' where the melee spills out into Pall Mall (p 144); and of the wax-model of 'Samuel Johnson's Literary Club' meeting in the Turks' Head tavern (p 119). Gatrell cites a 1789 listing of fifty 'convivial societies', including the Druids, the Old Codgers, the Independent Codgers, the Nose Club, and the Fumblers: 'Men went to clubs like these to get drunk and to talk dirty…' (p 120). The chamber-pot resided in the same sideboard from which dinner was served, and would be used openly as necessary – which must have been frequently given the quantum of wine and spirits consumed; a volume only matched by the gambling losses sustained by gentlemen young and old (Beau Brummell amassed debts of £50,000 at his club; Fox £11,000 in one session). For a vivid description of London life in the eighteenth-century see Ackroyd (2016, chapter 14) as the world of Smollett's 'Humphrey Clinker', of Hogarth's 'Moll Hackabout' and of his 'Gin Lane' (there being an estimated 8500 gin-shops), of Fielding's 'Tom Jones', of rampant crime and of ubiquitous beggars as the back-drop for the contrasting grandeur of the British Museum opened in 1759 and the Royal Academy opened in 1768.

And libertine clubs were to be found beyond London – the 'Monks' or Hellfire Club of Sir Francis Dashwood at Medmenham Abbey is well-known, but the Beggar's Benison of Anstruther rather less so even if it appears for a century it got up to much the same antics (Gatrell, 2006, pp 312/3). See also Jones (1943) on 'The Clubs of the

Georgian Rakes'; and Lord (2008) on the Hell-Fire Clubs. On the dandy, from Brummell to Beerbohm, see Moers (1960) – George Bryan Brummell (1778-1840), aka Beau Brummell, Eton and the Hussars, 'leader of fashion in London', died in the asylum in Caen (the *DNB*); Sir Henry Maximilian ('Max') Beerbohm (1872-1956), Charterhouse and Merton, 'the best essayist, parodist, and cartoonist of his age', author of *Zuleika Dobson* (the *DNB*). But, of course, the riotous Georgian age gave way to the primness of Victorian London, not least as great chunks of the inner core of the city were redeveloped and gentrified (and our Pall Mall Clubhouses built): 'Materially, topographically, as well as culturally, we witness the coming of a more socially differentiated, ordered and decorous world.' (Gatrell, 2006, p 595). On Georgian 'Fashionable Society' see Greig (2013); on Brummell, dandyism, and the Savile Row gentlemen's suit, see Breward (2016).

Dr Johnson's propensity for founding clubs is chronicled by Bingham, 2010, in an essay on 'Clubs and Clubbability' (pp 33-46), noting that Johnson in his 'Dictionary' defined 'club' as 'an assembly of good fellows, meeting under certain conditions'. His first club was the Ivy Lane Club (1749), his next became his most famous as The Club (1764, aka The Literary Club from 1779), and later came the Essex Head Club (1783). In commenting on the merits of various individuals for membership of such clubs Johnson commented that one was 'a most unclubbable man' while of another that he was 'a very clubbable man' thus adding two new words to the English language, albeit that neither appears in Johnson's own dictionary. His second creation, 'The Club', survives: its 1905 History listed 233 members since 1764, 'all but eight appearing in the *Dictionary of National Biography* '; it met at various places over the centuries, most recently at Brooks's. It is this Club that Paxman (1990, p 314/5) calls 'the most exclusive dining club in Britain' with a membership of just over fifty as 'precisely the sort of cast-list you'd come up with if you were looking for the heart of the Establishment: powerful, well-upholstered men confident in their authority... [albeit that this membership] has a slightly ancient regime feel'. Cannadine (2017, p 328) comments on the powerful, interconnected, and elite 1850s membership of 'The Club' – a membership overlapping with that of the Athenaeum which, among 'the mid-Victorian proliferation of dining clubs and literary societies', in its heyday 'was the most famous and significant' (p 321).

A study of London's Augustan clubs by a Harvard academic (Allen, 1933) talks of 'the extraordinary rise of the club' and the popularity of 'the practice of clubbing', their meetings being held in taverns and coffee-houses: Pepys, for instance, records in his 'Diary' on 9th January 1660 attending in 'the Coffee Club' a meeting of the Rota Club and having paid '18d to be entered' for a discussion on 'the state of the Roman government'; and on 3rd February 1664 he is at Will's Coffee-house for a 'very witty and pleasant discourse' with 'all the wits of the town'. By the 1700s Allen describes the 'Kit-Cats and Toasters' emerging as Whig political clubs, to be followed by 'the Calves-Head Club' and 'the Mug-House Clubs'; but countered by 'Swift's Tory Clubs' and 'the October Club' (also the Scribblers Club formed in 1714 from the earlier Society of Brothers: Ackroyd, 2016, pp 67/68) – all part of 'the new social phenomenon' that also included disorderly clubs catering for rakes, the 'Mohocks' and the 'Hell-Fires'. Calmer times eventually ensued by way of debating societies/clubs such as the Robin Hood Society (1747), and slowly these clubs of various kinds (political, literary, scientific, philosophical, gambling, arts) began the transition to having their own exclusive premises (White's first, then Brooks's and Boodle's setting the trend). Club-life started to be portrayed and indeed satirised in 'The Tatler' and in 'The Spectator', the latter inventing 'the Ugly Club of Oxford' and 'the Everlasting Club' (at least two of its members always being gathered). Another satire on the 'London Clubs' by Ward (1709, aka 'The London Spy' – and in many editions subsequently) has inter alia: the Lying Club, the Thieves' Club, the Beggars' Club, the Broken Shop-keepers' Club, the No Nose Club, the Quacks' Club, the Mollies' Club (this last having members 'degenerated from all Masculine Deportment or Manly Exercises') – for more on Ward see Lord, 2008, pp 21-24.

Ross (1976) puts the evolution of London's clubs in a wider historical and geographical context, considering the development of 'voluntary association' in 'Primitive Societies', in 'Ancient Societies', in the guilds and the fraternities of the Middle Ages, and so to 'English Clubs and Social Change' as the 'religious fraternity' gave way to the 'secular club' based on 'the ideal-typical club member' as 'the gentleman' – 'a prodigy of hedonism' seeking to counter his problem of ennui (Bertie Wooster!), in search of a life and a social focus (The Drones Club!) that could not be a guild or livery company (Palfreyman, 2010) and nor a fraternity or sect: the club became a simpler model for sociability, close to the *hetairia* of Ancient Greece or to certain forms of the *collegia* in Ancient Rome. The first may have been the Court of Good Company founded by Occleve (or Hoccleve, c1369-c1426) in the early-1400s; the next probably founded by Raleigh (c1552-1618) in 1603; and 'the dawn of a new phase in club life' following as the coffee-houses developed from the 1650s/60s, as already discussed, and from which our more or less respectable gentlemen's clubs eventually emerged and indeed generally flourished into this new century (albeit with a few casualties along the way).

In Clark (2000) we get another detailed study of the pre-1800 clubs, of 'an Associational World' - such clubs being seen from the start as 'a distinctly British phenomenon' and giving rise to 'a distinctive pattern of associational activity in the Anglophone world' (p 5). He notes as a subset of such activity the emergence during the Restoration decades of the SCR in the Oxford colleges as 'a social club for dons separate from the college's administration' (as indeed is still the case – except that annual subscriptions are no longer paid by the modern don, whose level of poverty is exceeded only by a taste for costly coffee-machines...): Merton led the way in 1661, as noted by the ubiquitous antiquarian Anthony Wood (1632-1695). Clark sees clubs of various kinds maturing into 'a national social institution' over the period 1688-1760, and Our Clubs emerging as a strand within this social trend: he estimates there were some 6500 clubs across 'the English-speaking World' by 1799 (p 128) compared to barely 100 a century before.

This expansion as 'the growth of public sociability' was stimulated by urbanisation and by the development of newspapers, while not being impeded by Government's bungling attempts periodically to suppress such gatherings (the rulers of Ancient Rome were rather more effective at banning clubs or collegia as 'political and social dangers in the republican city' (Lane Fox, 2005, p 480); as indeed were continental dictators such as Napoleon, setting the tone for the restrictiveness of civil code nations compared to the common law countries such as England and America – one of the many factors in the UK, or at least England, not being at ease with EU membership and hence the 2016 BREXIT vote: Tombs, 2014, p 878). At the same time the number of Freemasons Lodges grew from 4 to 93 in London alone, and to 263 elsewhere in the UK (Clark, 2000, p 310). Thus, in late-Georgian society: 'Clubbing extended its influence well beyond the metropolitan smart classes' (p 430), creating a 'networking universe' that 'acted to counter those pressures of social fragmentation which were spawned by rapid urbanisation' (p 449). Britain became 'an associational society' and 'a networked nation' with all these clubs and societies promoting 'the steady accumulation of social capital' and 'a more open and pluralistic society' (p 469). Ackroyd (2016, pp 107-109) writes of 'the notable emergence of clubs as the medium of male exchange' – 'The clubs were intended to foster cheerfulness and conviviality, friendship and mutual understanding… Clubs were now to be found everywhere.'. On another manifestation of social activity see Girouard (1990, chapter 7, 'The Assembly Rooms') concerning subscriptions to regular 'seasons' of 'assemblies' in the fashionable and plush assembly rooms opened in towns all over England from the early decades of the eighteenth-century to the middle of the nineteenth-century – and, of course, most notably in Bath. Similarly, Philippson (2011) comments on the 'civil infrastructure' of eighteenth-century cities: 'a culture that revolved around societies of men of letters, dedicated to the improvement of literature, philosophy, natural science and the fine and useful arts; small informal clubs… meeting in coffee-houses and taverns – and attempting to combine polite conversation with serious drinking…' (p 78).

Finally, before we move into the nineteenth-century as the key period for the evolution of Our Clubs, of their Clubhouses, and of Clubland, it is interesting to note that the coffee-houses and taverns era earns a whole 7 pages of a mere 376 covering the entire global history of mankind in 'A Concise History of THE WORLD' (Wiesner-Hanks, 2015). The section entitled 'Drug Foods and Commercialisation' (pp 243-250) gives a summary, but on a global basis, of what is set out above for the London of c1650-1750. Thus, 'caffeinated-beverages' become popular as coffee spreads from its native Ethiopia to Yemen around 1400 and then across the Muslim world, drunk 'primarily in coffeehouses that served as places of male sociability'. The Europeans duly learn about coffee from the Ottomans, but it was too expensive until the Dutch grew it on a large scale in their colonies within Asia and South America (notably on Java). By the 1650s/1660s coffee-houses are springing up in Vienna, London, Paris, and other European cities as 'places where (mostly) men gathered to talk about business, politics, or whatever' – and hence rulers, 'from Sultan Murad IV (r. 1623-40) of the Ottoman Empire to King Charles II of Britain (ruled 1660-85) attempted periodically to close them down as they worried about sedition'.

These venues became part of the emerging 'public sphere' where a new political force of 'public opinion' was developing through the 'discussion clubs' held on their premises – such clubs 'were founded in many cities across Europe, including Paris, Edinburgh, London, Naples, Rome, and Warsaw, and across the Atlantic in the British, French, and Spanish colonies'. Similarly, tea – as another 'drug' – spread from China via Japan and Korea into Europe, and became the 'female sociability around a teapot' response to the role coffee played in the male sociability of the coffee-house. And, of course, another drug was alcohol – notoriously gin in eighteenth-century London – as well as tobacco, and also opium (often taken mixed with alcohol as laudanum); all three featured globally in what Wiesner-Hanks sees as: 'A new world of connections, 1500CE-1800CE' (Chapter 4).

So, we have an eighteenth-century London with its taverns that would have been familiar to Falstaff, its coffee-houses, its ladies taking tea in their salons, its gin-shops and gin-palaces, and its new Clubs (Boodle's, 1762; Brooks's, 1764; White's, 1736) – as well indeed its expanding theatre-land. By the time we leave the Victorian period at the end of the next section of this Chapter our Clubland will have blossomed and the first of the great hotels with their famous restaurants will have come on the scene as a competitor (the Langham, 1865; the Savoy, 1889; Claridge's, 1898; the Ritz, 1906) – but the gin-palaces and the coffee-houses will have faded away (the latter revived as 'coffee public houses' promoted in the 1870s as an alternative to pubs and then, of course, destined to reappear in the 1990s/2000s with a vengeance as Starbucks, Nero, and Costa outlets). The opium dens known to Sherlock Holmes, Edwin Drood, and Dorian Gray will also have disappeared, their East End sites now blocks of Thames-side 'from £1m' apartments; and likewise the music-halls will have come and gone between c1850 and c1960 (Max Miller died in 1963). Our Clubs, however, with their history of almost three hundred years stretching across four centuries - from the eighteenth-century White's established in 1736, via their expansion during the nineteenth-century and taking in also their varying fortunes during the twentieth-century, and so up to today in a new century – have largely survived over this long period and indeed now even thrive, despite concern about their economic viability in the Edwardian era and despite a spate of closures and mergers post-War and into the 1960s/1970s.

VICTORIAN CLUBLAND AND ITS CLUBS

Porter (1994, pp 281/2) provides a neat assessment of the growth of nineteenth-century Clubland: the Clubs were 'exclusive', the Athenaeum being judged by one foreign observer as 'the last word of a high civilisation' while another commentator saw 'the improvement and multiplication of the Clubs' as 'the grand feature of metropolitan progress' for within them 'a man of moderate habits can dine more comfortably for three or four shillings (including half a pint of wine) than he could have dined for four or five times that amount at the coffee houses and hotels, which were [hitherto] the habitual resort of the bachelor class'. Yet the married chaps were also flocking to the Clubs – leading some critics to worry about their lavishness engendering 'the cult of egotism, the abandonment of family virtues, the exclusive taste for material pleasures, and a deplorable laxity of morals of which the whole nation will someday feel the baneful consequences'. Such concerns were a tad overblown: while the Georgian clubs had been gambling-dens, the Victorian 'new models were solid, sober, even stuffy; they kept up appearances'. That said, Machray (1902) gives an account of late nights in the racier of Our Clubs: Chapter XI on 'Club Life', Chapter XII on 'A Saturday Night with the Savages' (at the Savage Club), and Chapter XIII 'With the Eccentrics at 3 am'.

Porter (1994) continues: 'Indeed they *had* impressive appearances. The United Service Club of 1827, designed by Nash and sited at the corner of Waterloo Place and Pall Mall East, was the first of a series of grand clubhouses to sprout up in the area' (now the Institute of Directors HQ) – John Nash (1752-1835), his works include laying out Regent's Park, planning Regent Street, enlarging Buckingham Palace, but his style 'lacks grandeur' (from his entry in the *DNB* as another great piece of scholarship, like the *OED*, from Oxford University – we, of course, await anything similar from The Other Place!). The Athenaeum was to a Grecian design by Decimus Burton (1800-1881) and was begun in 1830; the Travellers' Club (1829-31) was the work of Sir Charles Barry (1795-1860) to resemble an Italian palazzo; and Barry also built the Reform (1837-41) with its façade based on the Farnese Palace in Rome (in addition Barry was the architect of Bridgewater House as well as the Houses of Parliament).

These Clubs 'spanned the private and public spheres, while upholding rank and exclusivity' – and, as a Frenchman observed, avoided the Englishman encountering the unrestrained gaiety of and the presence of women in the Paris café. These 'Clubs helped keep London a masculine city, and St James's, with its bachelor chambers around King and Jermyn Streets, was its inner sanctum.' Thus, the gentlemen-adventurers, Hannay and Carruthers, are unsurprisingly found languishing in their Clubs at the start of the famous novels by, respectively, Buchan and Childers – see Chapter II. As Porter notes, it is a bit of a contrast with the Victorian suburbs where we find London's 'representative middle-class mascot' in the form of Charles Pooter (George and Weedon Grossmith, *Diary of a Nobody*); still more with the lives of those further down the socio-economic hierarchy depicted by Charles Dickens or Henry Mayhew. That said, Pooter did get to dine at 'The Constitutional', invited by his friend, Frenching; and on another occasion he gets sozzled on Champagne of such good quality that the supply is usually 'entirely bought up by a West-end club'.

Underwood (1998, pp 646-8) notes that the nineteenth-century gentlemen's clubs were 'exclusive, but not especially expensive'; and that by 1900 London had 'around 100 clubs' (including eight for the military, five for university graduates, and nine for women). Picard (2005, pp 57 & 104/5) comments on their 'grandiloquent buildings' as 'the stately procession of gentlemen's clubs in or near Pall Mall', all as 'monuments of the Victorian way of life'. She also notes how women's magazines lamented these Clubs as places that potential husbands escaped to 'like shy animals, vanishing when hotly pursued' (as one article expressed the problem). Some, however, argued in reply that the Clubs trained and prepared chaps as husbands-to-be, inducing habits of economy and sobriety. These 'comfortable male hideouts' had wash-basins in the bedrooms and at the Reform Club even 'a captive gas flame in a little alcove by the main door, at which gentlemen could light their cigars' (similarly the Army and Navy Club, opened in 1851, had twenty lines of 'Wishaw's Telekouphona or Speaking Telegraph' which enabled the Club Secretary to communicate with various bits of his empire) . Under such circumstances marriage could safely be delayed until the early-thirties before the attraction of clubbing faded. Such a shift from the eighteenth-century clubs as the venues for 'wild hedonism' to Victorian gentility (albeit not in all Clubs) was influenced by the Duke of Wellington, looking to create suitable recreational zones to keep military officers out of mischief: the Duke, in helping found at least three Clubs, provided timeless sound advice – 'Buy the freehold... [and] if you let in the bishops, mind your umbrellas'.

Thus, a 'character' of Victorian London in Mayhew's 'London Characters' is this bachelor gent, perhaps 'a Foreign office clerk [on his way to eventually being an ambassador somewhere insignificant within the Empire] a rather weak-headed young gentleman, of very good family and very poor fortune... His views, at present, are limited to his office, the 'Times', his club, and any shootings and fishings...'. And indeed having a Club address could be played upon to advantage: 'In nothing should a man who means to be in society in London be so scrupulous about as his address...' ('Blackwood's Magazine', 1841). If a chap can't manage 'Lower Mount Street', a posh Club will do. But, that said, beware the recent 'custom of giving cards from clubs... you must always avoid fellows who give you a card, not of their residence, but of their club; depend upon it, the leprosy of poverty hangs about these fellows...'.

Our gracious Club buildings, filled with 'weak-headed' and impecunious bachelors as they may be, must not, of course, be confused with another physical manifestation of the English keenness to organise themselves into clubs: the 'club carriages' on the Victorian railways (Bradley, 2015, p 83). These were for the exclusive use of a named select group of commuters whose committee elected new members and, of course, drew up copious rules concerning the allocation of armchairs and the opening of windows. They seem to have been exclusively a Manchester phenomenon – from/to Blackpool, Windermere, and Llandudno (on the last route members had their own lockers and tea was served on the return journey home): 'The set-up is so like the premise of a P.G. Wodehouse story that it is a surprise to learn that gritty Manchester remained the only stronghold of these club trains, which never made the leap southward to the commuter-land of the Home Counties.'.

In thinking about Clubland in the Victorian era, there is also Milne-Smith (2011, with a usefully extensive Bibliography) who carefully explores the Clubs from the perspective of 'masculinity studies' as (according to the cover) the 'first scholarly history of the famed gentlemen's clubs of London' that 'takes us behind the majestic doors of these most exclusive clubs' in order to dissect 'a robust masculine culture in decline'. As Milne-Smith notes, 'Clubland was both an imagined community and a very real place' (p 5) – as the former, thanks to its portrayal in Victorian literature (see Black (2012) and the next Chapter), it was widely familiar. By the end of the Victorian period there were around 75 gentlemen's clubs in London, with membership varying from 350 to 2500, and thirty of these constitute Clubland-proper according to Milne-Smith's little map on p 33, as a collection of 'elite spaces' where membership confirmed and bestowed 'status' – and membership being jealously guarded by a rigorous election process, involving the deployment of black-balls and voting machines/boxes (one black-ball per ten or so voters meant social death for the aspirant gent having been 'black-balled' or 'pilled': a 'pill' being a boring chap) . If a bounder still manged to get past the election process, there were rules for expulsion from the Club - especially as expectations of decent behaviour increased and a gentleman's 'character' might be questioned for infelicities (and especially inebriation) ignored in the previous rather more rakish century. Incidentally, the term 'blackballing' comes from ancient Athens – a fragment of black pottery in the voting box meant banishment; the fragments were from tiles called 'ostrakans', and hence ostracism. Ballot relates to the Venetians casting their votes by placing different coloured 'ballotte' (small balls) in a bag. And so we get blackballing via a ballot of voting members in London Clubland as a rather later democratic process.

Milne-Smith further notes how these Clubs were 'emporia of gossip' of a male kind, based on competitive witticisms and *bons mots* (Chapter 4 on 'Club Talk') - and with wickedly scandalous gossip freely and enjoyably passed around within the Club but subject to a kind of Chatham House rules as to what leaked beyond the grand edifice and its 'lavish and well-appointed' interior that provided the domestic pleasures of club-life (Chaper 5 on 'The Club as Home' – the loss of which could be disconcerting, distressing, and disorientating during annual Club closures). And did the Clubs create self-centred and lazy men incapable of sustaining marital harmony? Certainly (as already noted above) there were critics concerned over 'The Bachelor 'Problem'' (Chapter 6), worried that men retreated to their Clubs and avoided the domestic hearth, but wider social changes meant that, while Bertie Wooster might thankfully escape from hectoring women by fleeing into the Drones' (see Chapter II), by the 1920s 'even Bertie Wooster spent more time in the company of women… than he did at the Drones' Club' (p 205): in short, the world changed and the Clubs with it on into the twentieth-century. The anti-women theme is picked up in the definition of 'Club' offered by Ambrose Bierce (an American journalist) in his 1911 'The Devil's Dictionary': 'An association of men for purposes of drunkenness, gluttony, unholy hilarity, murder, sacrilege and the slandering of mothers, wives and sisters.'.

Sticking with the (for this author at least, novel) idea of 'masculine studies', Barbara Black (2012) also explores Our Clubs as bolt-holes for chaps in the Victorian era (she being another female US academic, like Amy Milne-Smith above, seemingly fascinated by Clubland as a male citadel during the Golden Age of Clubs). They were 'a way of ordering and making sense of the world' (p 19) and became increasingly central to the upper-class male lifestyle as the nineteenth-century progressed: a statistical analysis (p 29) on the use of the word 'club' shows it peaking in the 1910s and again in the 1930s, while 'gentlemen's clubs' peaks around 2000 for, one suspects, reasons rather different... She cleverly notes that 'edifice envy' drove the competition to build increasingly grandiose Clubhouses, linking into 'the male culture of dominance, hierarchy, and scale' (p 75); and selects a fine 'pitch-perfect' quote from the prolific journalist Sala (pp 85/6) writing in 1859 on the Clubman: 'He is all of the club, and clubby. He is full of club matters, club gossip. He dabbles in club intrigues, belongs to certain club cliques, and takes part in club quarrels. No dinners are so good to him as the club dinners... he writes his letters on the club paper, pops them into club envelopes, seals them with the club seal... He is rather sorry that there is no club uniform. He would like when he dies, to be buried in a club coffin, in the club cemetery, and to be followed to the grave by the club, with members of the committee as pall-bearers.'. George Augustus Sala, as already noted, was himself a great Clubman, belonging to the Beefsteak, the Reunion, and the Reform, as well as helping launch the Savage Club.

Black also comments on a range of periodicals that portrayed Clubland: the well-known and wide-ranging *Pall Mall Gazette* and *Punch*, but also lesser-known and often very short-lived dedicated ones such as *Club Chat*, *Club News*, *Clubland*, and *Echoes from the Clubs* – their style was like a celebrity magazine today, the last seeking to capture 'the sparkling waifs and strays' associated with Clubland while also ensuring that its 'latest *bon mot* and *repartee* will be echoed to the world'. Digging out from the stacks of the Bodleian Library the mere three issues of *Clubland* that it possesses, we find it was a 6d monthly publication edited by P. Gordon Bamber, whose first editorial (May 1910) pledged it would 'chronicle the inner life and happiness of our London clubs' since

'Club life is the quintessence of our British temperament'. Thus, there were sections such as 'Round the Clubs' offering Clubland gossip, 'Fixtures of the Month' re Clubland events, 'Biographical Sketches' of prominent Clubland members (the initial one being the King), and a 'Clubland's Short Story'; while beyond the narrow focus of Clubland there were 'Trips Abroad', 'The Horse and Course', 'The Japan-British Exhibition', 'Golf', 'The Motorist and the Car', 'The Universities' (ie sport at Oxford and Cambridge, ignoring the likes of the newly-established Manchester University and Birmingham University), and 'Society Small-talk'. It was lamented that 'The Bohemian Clubs of London' were now reduced to mainly the Savage Club and the Eccentrics compared to the heady days of half a century earlier; and it helpfully corrected the wicked rumour, 'owing to a misunderstanding', that the New Oxford and Cambridge Club was about to be taken over by the American Universities Club. All in all one can see why it may have ceased publication after Issue No. 3.

Non-members must have read these Clubland magazines if they were to be commercially viable (even briefly), demonstrating the abiding external interest in what Sala ('Clubbism is a great mystery') saw as the intriguing allure of the Clubs for those standing outside in Pall Mall and having no chance of getting past the Hall Porter to storm the grand staircase to the smoking-room or the bar. And even in the 1960s/1970s there could be a popular TV comedy sitcom series set inside the London Club – the fictional 'Imperial' of *Bootsie and Snudge* to (see Chapter II). So, according to Black, we should see the Victorian period and its 'club culture [as] a uniquely British [nay, English!] form that achieved high purpose and identity', where 'Victorian gentlemen's clubs were a product of, and a force for, their time' in helping forge 'a corporate identity of Englishness' for a certain male socio-economic strata (pp 234/5): see also Tosh (1999/2007) on the Club as a feature of Victorian masculinity. Similarly Doughan & Gordon (2006) view the history of clubs ('an example of Anglo-Saxon exotica', p 7) as being 'based on two ancient British ideas – the segregation of the classes, and the segregation of the sexes' (p 15), women being the key category 'for exclusion' (p 4). They comment, however, that, interestingly, Almack's Rooms (1765) was mixed, the male members selecting female members and vice versa; while in the past twenty years they note that several Private Members Bills in the Commons designed to outlaw single-sex clubs have been blocked. Their chapter 4 discusses such Victorian women-only clubs as the Lyceum Club and the Pioneer Club, with the Minerva Club of the 1920s being very feminist; the 'flourishing' survivor they note as the University Women's Club. More (1908) is a long moan about being 'the victim of what may reasonably be called a conspiracy' whereby the author, as 'a campaigner in Ladies Clubs', bought 'a derelict Ladies' Club' in 1904 but could not make it economically viable because of the antics of various (female) members trying to thwart her.

On the expansion of Clubland in the later decades of the nineteenth-century see Taddei (1999) concerning the role of the Clubs in providing scope for networking ('the club played the role of an information hub') and also for establishing status – Taddei estimates that the total membership of Our Clubs by the 1890s and 1900s may have exceeded 100,000 (sic!) – Girtin (1964, p 57) talks of 'some 200,000'. This Victorian fixation with social status and the burnishing of it through membership of the right Club(s) explains the focus on the election process for membership and all the endless anecdotes about 'black-balling' and 'pilling'. Thus, the Club Rules would be very clear on the election mechanism, as these examples illustrate: from the Athenaeum in 1862 whose Rule III envisaged a periodic Ballot of all Members where 'one black ball in ten shall exclude' a proposed and seconded applicant listed in 'the Proposing Book'; while the Army and Navy Club Rules 6-8 stipulated that names in 'the Candidate-book' will be balloted monthly among all Members, again with 'one black ball in ten to exclude'. In contrast, the Edinburgh Piobaireachd Society left elections to membership to 'be determined by a majority of those present of the Committee' – this august Society existed (and still exists) for 'the encouragement, study, and playing of Piobaireachd on the Highland Bagpipe' and for 'the general advancement and diffusion of knowledge of the ancient Highland Piobaireachd'. Likewise, the Lansdowne Club Rules in 2011 shift the task of 'Membership and Election thereto' from the entire membership to the elected Council: 'The Council may elect or refuse to elect as they think fit.' – but balls may still be needed and perhaps even a voting-machine into which they can be dropped ('Should the election be by ballot, two black balls shall exclude.').

Finally, before we enter the twentieth-century: The most compelling and detailed case for the Establishment role of Our Clubs, at least in mid-Victorian times, is made in Thevoz (2018). He explores the development of the 'political' Clubs (the Tories at the Carlton from 1832 and the Liberals from 1836 in the Reform) along with the membership of such Clubs (and of others) among MPs as part of 'the living patterns of Victorian legislators' (some 90% belonged to a Club). Today's Clubs as the homes of (what he terms in rather un-academic language) collectives of 'clapped-out old farts' are very different from 'their Victorian heyday' when they (or their members) exercised 'unprecedented power and influence' (the phrase 'club government' being invented in 1836 – cf 'sofa government' in the Blair era). And these MP members certainly made full use within their 'networks' of 'the geography of space' by way of Club meeting rooms and also (for the exchange of gossip) social/dining/bar facilities, all, of course, as spaces carefully guarded by the Hall Porter against any attempted intrusions by the Public. But the Public seemed to recognise what went on in the Clubs and hence they were occasionally 'a suitable focus of public protest' as the marchers passed along Pall Mall. The Clubs even had Commons division bells installed by the 1850s and presumably MPs were duly to be spied sprinting between Pall Mall and the House.

OUR CLUBS IN THE TWENTIETH-CENTURY

As Kinnear (1902) notes, at the start of the twentieth-century, 'No city in the world has so many clubs as London' – all located in 'a zig-zag course' that is 'Clubland' and that is centred on the 'almost imperial' Pall Mall (see Burford, 1988, on the whole area of St James's). It is no accident that in the early years of the century we see three significant publications on the Clubland and Clubmen, and indeed these are the only substantial broad studies of the Clubs phenomenon before this modest offering a century later: Griffiths (1907), Nevill (1911), and Escott (1914). In between the Clubs, as can be seen in Chapter II in terms of their portrayal in literature, came to be seen, accurately or not, as part of the centre of power and influence within English politics and society, as part of the mid-century fixation with identifying 'the Establishment' and locating its haunts.

So, were the Clubs really a key element in the life of 'the Establishment'? The short *OED* definition of 'Establishment' is: 'social group exercising authority or influence, and generally seeking to resist changes'; while *Encarta* has: 'a group of people who hold power in a society or social group and dominate its institutions'. The full *OED* gives us: 'a social group exercising power generally, or within a given field or institution, by virtue of its traditional superiority, and by the use esp. of tacit understandings and often a common mode of speech, and having as a general interest the maintenance of the status quo' (with uses cited from

1936, 1945, 1955 (ie Fairlie as below), 1957, 1958 (C.P. Snow), 1959…).

Thus, we have the concept of the Establishment as peopled by powerful and influential folk, possessing a sense of entitlement and linked by a common dress code as well as a style of speech, who progress serenely through life on a pre-determined fixed path: independent schooling to acquire the Old School Tie, next Oxford & Cambridge colleges, thence the Inns of Court or the City or Whitehall (perhaps even MI5/6), finally membership of a Club or two – the Establishment of the 1950s? Sandbrook (2005, pp 560-8) reminds us that A.J.P. Taylor, the seemingly non-establishment Oxford don, first coined the term in 1953 for 'the anachronistic, snobbish, conspiratorial political elite' as an old-boy network (what the nineteenth-century radical reformer William Cobbett had termed 'the THING'): 'The Establishment draws in recruits from outside as soon as they are ready to conform to its standards and become respectable. There is nothing more agreeable in life than to make peace with the Establishment – and nothing more corrupting.' (Taylor in the *New Statesman*). It was thus in 1955 that Henry Fairlie in the *Spectator* (23/9/1955) used the term for what he described as 'the matrix of official and social relations by which power is exercised'. Sandbrook notes that, between 1956 and 1961, certain Oxbridge colleges 'were especially successful at sending boys to fill senior positions within the civil service' – 27 from New College, 26 from King's, 25 from Balliol: a theme stressed by Ellis (1994) on 'The Oxbridge Conspiracy'. This was 'Our Age' (Noel Annan's 1990 retrospective examination of public affairs during his lifetime), as caught by such fiction as Anthony Powell's collection of novels 'Dance to the Music of Time' (1951-75) or C.P. Snow's series of novels studying the corridors of power ('Strangers and Brothers', 1940-70): this, in Sandbrook's words, 'a cloistered, successful, masculine and exclusive environment'.

Hugh Thomas's edited collection of essays on 'The Establishment' (1959) saw it as 'the present day institutional museum of Britain', featuring the Public Schools (which should be 'completely swept away'), the Army, the BBC, the City, and the Civil Service – but did not directly implicate Our Clubs. Anthony Sampson, however, in the first of his long-running series 'Anatomy of Britain' (1962) called for the country to rid itself of 'the club-amateur outlook' (p 638). And also in 1962 he commented: 'Still pillars of the English way of life, they are being nibbled by two sets of termites – women and businessmen' ('Harper's Magazine', November '62, 'The Mystique of British Clubs'). The satire vogue of the early-1960s ('Beyond the Fringe', 'That Was The Week That Was' ('TW3'), 'Private Eye') also created in 1961 'The Establishment' on Greek Street as Peter Cook's satirical cabaret club, its main target being Prime Minister 'Never Had It So Good' Macmillan – by 1964 it had fallen prey to Soho racketeering and 'was effectively being run by gangsters' (Sandbrook, 2005, pp 570-93) – a fate to which none of Our Clubs has seemingly, so far, succumbed.

All this will have been at a time that the 'Beast of Bolsover' was forming his socialist and anti-Establishment perspective on the world: in 'The New Book of Snobs: A definitive guide to modern snobbery' (D.J. Taylor, 2016, pp 121-127) the veteran Labour MP, Dennis Skinner, is listed as one of the 'inverted snobs' – 'seeing snobbery where none is intended'. There is a quote from Skinner's autobiography on his contemplating the 'Who's Who' form as a newly-elected MP in the 1970s: 'I realised this section was the place to list the Pall Mall boltholes of a ruling class, the posh centres of power where a tiny, wealthy, privileged elite endured, over gin-and-tonics served to them by liveried flunkies as they luxuriated in deep leather armchairs…'. One wonders whether Our Clubs after around 250 years of adapting, and indeed the Livery Companies or the Oxbridge colleges after some 750 years of surviving Henry VIII and

Cromwell as well as Hitler, would be allowed to survive a Corbyn truly socialist Labour government were the nation so unwise to elect one… quaint, quirky, quintessentially English institutions as quarry to be hunted out of existence as the Brave New World beckons?

That the Establishment met at Our Clubs is supposedly revealed by the frequent need for lunches, drinks, and dinners at the Athenaeum for the top fictional civil servants in Lynn & Jay's sublime 'Yes Minister' and 'Yes Prime Minister'. And, as Sandbrook (2015, pp 252/3) notes, it is also the same for our top fictional spies: 'In his political and social conservatism, Bond conforms absolutely to type… the character owed a good deal to the 'clubland heroes' of the interwar years… Typically they took on Jews, Communists and Russians in various combinations… The job done, they retired to their West End clubs: fortress of masculine endeavour, enclaves of sanity in a changing world, with no women to spoil the atmosphere and a reliable porter to guard the gate… If Bond has a vision of paradise, it is Blades, the gentlemen's club where he dines with M at the beginning of *Moonraker*. Fleming based it largely on his own club, Boodle's.'. Sandbrook also notes that in one of the Boulting brothers 1950s often anti-Establishment Ealing comedies, 'I'm All Right Jack' (Peter Sellers as the trade unionist, Fred Kite), the first scene is 'set in a gentlemen's club on VE Day': (in Sandbrook's words) 'A servant goes to wake 'old Sir John', to tell him that the war is over at last. But the narrator warns, change is coming. 'Look hard', he says, 'for this is the last we will see of Sir John… a solid block in the edifice of what seemed to be an ordered and stable society. There goes Sir John – on his way out.' (pp 444/5).

Paxman (1990, Chapter 13, 'Bring on the Comfortable Men') notes how to many of his generation certain anonymous buildings in Pall Mall and St James's 'seemed to be the secret seat of British power' (the Clubs do not, as also for the Oxbridge colleges, have nameplates

– if you should be there, you will know where they are; if you do not belong, you do not need their location identified!). These grand edifices had 'high windows through which one could glimpse the gilt-framed portraits of Empire heroes and white-coated waiters serving coffee to balding heads in armchairs'. Yet, as he notes, by the 1960s and 1970s, membership was falling and dozens 'closed their doors and sold up' (perhaps eighty between the War and 1980 – see the Appendices for the List of Clubs Past and for the amalgamations recorded in the List of Clubs Present). In the immediate decades post-War the Clubs may well have 'had entirely the wrong image for the age of the Common Man', and perhaps Macmillan and Rab Butler's generation of politicians were the last for whom 'the London clubs were just part of life'.

Twenty-five years on from this Paxman analysis the surviving Clubs seem to be doing well, not least 'by sacking the mad majors who had until then [the 1980s] acted as secretaries and engaging catering managers' (much as Oxbridge colleges 'professionalised' their bursarial functions in recent decades – for instance, the New College Fellow acting part-time as the Camerarius in the 1950s is replaced by the full-time employee Domestic Bursar by the 1970s, who is now the Home Bursar as also a Fellow alongside the full-time (Estates) Bursar that in the mid-1960s had already replaced the don previously managing the endowment assets on a part-time basis). Thus, for Paxman, the surviving Clubs remain as 'the pinnacle of a culture, from the public schools through the professions to the judiciary and parliament'; but 'only the conspiracist [sic] would argue that there was anything sinister about these gatherings' of clubbable chaps within Our Clubs. These Clubs are now 'no more than occasionally convenient watering holes for powerful men who are uneasy in pubs', for their influence is 'altogether more subtly conservative' than being the focus of 'a Capitalist Class' or 'a

Ruling Class' or 'a Power Elite' as detectors of conspiracy would have it.

One such locator of wicked conspiracy, however, is Scott (1991, Chapter 5, 'Is there still an Upper Circle?'): the public schools, the Oxbridge colleges, and 'the 'private' gentlemen's clubs' were linked as the 'old boy network', with the last providing 'a venue at which the connections which had been made at school and university could be renewed, reinforced, and elaborated'. Thus, for Scott, while their role 'as centres for meetings and intrigue' may have 'become a little less important than formerly', they are still part of the Establishment infrastructure, membership of which 'is simply a necessary badge of status and acceptance' within this Establishment, this Capitalist Class, this Ruling Class, this Power Elite (Reader, this is you!): 'To have a full collection of membership cards, like having a wallet full of credit cards, is a sign of membership in the upper circles.'. Yet, as Scott notes and as Paxman comments, 'such a person will often have better places to spend much of his time' (Scott) and 'most people are just too busy to spend as much time in clubs as they used to' (Paxman, who adds that anyway people's values are more individualistic 'and they have less time for the virtues of solidarity, companionship, clubbiness'). Figure 5.1 in the Scott book shows sixteen 'Principal London clubs' (supposedly 'ranked by fees' from the expensive Boodle's and Brooks's via the middling Athenaeum and Savile to the dirt-cheap National Liberal) – the Oxford and Cambridge is not even listed and, as a member, I have to assume this means that despite my 'Power Elite' pretensions, sadly, I am not after all part of that 'Upper Circle'! In contrast to Scott, Harrison (2010, p 138) declares that the Establishment, at least in the form of an influential upper socio-economic elite, by 1990 'had been retreating for some time'.

Indeed, there is the interesting possibility that the Establishment has not simply relocated from Our Clubs over recent decades (assuming it ever really operated a slick dominance from their dining-room tables over the claret and port), but has in fact just disintegrated. Davis (2018) sees the post-War Elite/Establishment (as described in such as Mills, 1956) as having lost the plot, as 'destabilised and disoriented', as 'precarious and rootless', as no longer 'in charge': there is a lack of expertise, of coherence, of vision, and of any sense of public service; there is only a loose collective of 'reckless opportunists' muddling and bluffing their way through while pursuing 'venal self-interest' (space to enter the politician(s) of choice: ....). He views the Halcyon Days of the Establishment as when it was a tight group sharing common experiences – including being 'members of expensive London clubs': 'The automatic links between exclusive education, tradition, status, power and money, which once typified the Establishment, have been broken. A far smaller percentage of those in power have taken the Clarendon [posh private schools]-Oxbridge [colleges] conveyor belt to the top. Exclusive London clubs lie empty or, worse still for elites, now allow women, foreigners, and lower-class members to join.' (pp 11 & 16).

A.N. Wilson (2005) comments on how the Trollopian Church of England remained outwardly unchanged on into the pre-War years within the sheltered atmosphere of 'Victorian clubland'. Noting that Trollope had decided to kill off Mrs Proudie as soon as possible after 'overhearing two old club [clergymen] bores talking of his fictional battleaxe' in the Athenaeum (as described in Chapter 15 of Trollope, *An Autobiography*), Wilson writes that 'had he returned to Earth in 1934, Trollope would have found the Athenaeum ['a place of limitless dullness'] full of characters from his novels – bishops in frock-coats, their top hats adorned with rosettes and rigging; club servants in livery. So little had changed.' (pp 310-312). This was indeed precisely the criticism levelled by Correlli Barnett (1995) also about 'the civil-service elite' in the immediate aftermath of the War: 'This elite being a stem of the liberal Establishment' spent their working-lives 'inside the sheltered habitat of the offices and committee rooms of Whitehall and Westminster and the duller clubs of Pall Mall – a kind of extended 'Fuhrer-bunker' the isolating nature of which was disguised by grand trappings.' (p 183).

The great explorer of the nooks and crannies inhabited by the English Establishment is, of course, Anthony Sampson in the six editions of his splendid 'Anatomy of Britain' (1962, 1965, 1971, 1982, 1992, 2004) and we can trace through the editions and the decades whether the Clubs are indeed part of the Establishment as, for example, Paxman and Scott suggest, for Sampson takes us 'on a guided tour of the galleries of power' with a view to determining 'who runs Britain?' (1971, p xvi). The 1965 edition has Chapter 4 (of 37 chapters) devoted to 'Clubs': 'The club is a pervading image among British institutions… and the London clubs are themselves an intrinsic part of the life of Whitehall… Viewed from the outside, the clubs have an air of infinite mystery… Clubs are an unchallenged English invention… The mystique of clubs…'. But: 'What does the influence of clubs amount to?' – they 'provide a useful venue for intrigue'; the Reform is 'the haunt of the Treasury' and the Travellers lunch-room is 'the Foreign Office Canteen' that is 'full of supercilious second secretaries', while 'the Athenaeum, for all its dignity, is not above intrigue… [where the Vice-Chancellors lobby] for university grants [and even] a very unclubbable breed [by way of] the scientists [duly] use it as a base for manoeuvre and fund-raising'.

Sampson poses the direct question: 'Is the future being settled among port and cigars in club chairs? Can membership confer a sliver of power?'. And he concludes that, even by the mid-1960s, the

Clubs were no longer quite as much a gallery of power as once they may have been: 'Perhaps there are still a few moments of intrigue when clubs are important. But while the reminiscences ramble on in Pall Mall, the future is being decided in the Cabinet Office canteen, in the directors' dining-room in ICI, or in the pubs round the corner from Transport House.'. Sampson in essence dismissed the concept of 'the Establishment', preferring to think in terms of 'a cluster of interlocking circles' of influence in corporatist and statist 1960s Britain. Indeed, he detects 'the crumbling of clubs' at least as somewhere the Establishment supposedly lurks and plots, schemes and connives; but, nevertheless, they 'will survive a long time, with their myths, their sites and the convenience' (although, as we have seen, many did indeed crumble in the 1970s). Sampson's 1962 first edition has pretty well the same 1965 wording for its Chapter 5 on 'Clubs' – a very short Chapter 4 on 'Land' had been dropped by the 1965 edition.

Guttsman (1963) reinforces Sampson, detecting a network of interlocking elite groups that, for instance, are used to staff influential and powerful bodies: 'Royal Commissions and Committee Chairmen are recruited predominantly from the ranks of the (upper) middle class... The majority of these 'honorary advisers' are [members of the Athenaeum or of the Reform], and, indeed, one cannot help thinking that membership of these two august bodies, to which so many of the chosen few belong, is conducive to selection. It is there and at the University Clubs that the selectors and selected meet.' (pp 351-353). A footnote points out that: 'Of the elite of the Civil Service [assessed as 73 bods]... 8 belong to the Athenaeum, 15 to the Reform Club and 22 to the University Clubs.'.

Harrison (2009, p 197), in his volume on Britain over the years 1950-1970, makes the same point as Sampson: he detects a 'dwindling national importance of London's Clubland' arising from 'fragmentation within the elite', Our Clubs 'becoming less central to the elite social round'. While Marwick (1998) in surveying 'The Sixties' sees the anti-Establishment attack from such as 'the Chelsea Set' on 'the old school tie' generation and on 'the old boy network' as part of a wider reaction against 'stuffy conventions and attitudes' (against 'squares') and less of an outright assault on 'the distribution of power as such', much as in the USA youth reacted against the 'Rat Race' (pp 56/57). The culmination was seen in the revolting students of 1968 as campus protest spread across the USA and (rather more amateurishly and less violently) within UK universities.

The 'Chivas Regal Book of London Clubs' (Graves, 1963) gives us a snapshot of the Clubs mid-century, some sixty of them (but including such as the City Livery and the Hurlingham beyond our Clubland proper). They are 'a purely English invention' – and one where 'Life is now catching up rapidly with Clubland' as Clubs battle to remain solvent, especially in the face of rising labour costs ('unless recourse is had to West Indians and other coloured servants') and with the risk that increased annual subscriptions trigger a mass exodus of members ('One West End club, which put up its subscription recently from 15 to 20 guineas, lost no fewer than 750 members.'). Hence, 'The death roll of clubs in recent years has indeed been formidable.' – the Marlborough, Orleans, Bachelors', Windham's (although the then members did get a 'bonus' of £400 each from its assets upon dissolution), Thatched House, Cocoa Tree, Conservative, 'and so many more' – because some were 'complacent', but not helped by the 'unkindness' of the Inland Revenue in recently deciding that Club subscriptions are not tax deductible. Thus, the 'Guardian' 928/4/1970) is quoted in the *OED* entry for 'club-land': 'SET [Selective Employment Tax] and rising land values in Central London are choking clubland like unwelcome smoke from a cheap cigar.'.

The book is of its time – the reference to 'coloured' staff and to staff being called 'servants'; as well as the misplaced confidence that 'there are never likely to be any' female members of the Athenaeum. The information on memberships and annual membership fees is interesting – for example, the Reform at £26 which is about £500 in 2016 prices with some 1650 members; the RAC at 20 guineas and with 15,000 members; Crockford's at 8 guineas and 'well over' 2,000 members; the Lansdowne at 35 guineas and 3,300 members; and the Number 10 Club with almost 36,000 members as the social centre of the Institute of Directors (5 guineas a year), where the bar 'is one of the finest in London' with a double dry martini for 4s and 6d and a Chivas Regal Whisky at 3s (c£4 and c£2.60 in today's prices) – the No10 duly went bust in 1975, perhaps indicating the same level of incompetence at running anything in the directorate level of British management that brought us British Leyland.

Finally, to put Our Clubs in context within post-War Britain, we can note from Sandbrook (2010, p 29) that they were (and still are? – see the Conclusion) an aspect 'of a nation obsessed with collective membership' (an obsession commented upon, as with have seen, in relation to the English and their penchant for clubs and associations in earlier times than the post-War decades). He comments that at the dawn of the 1970s 'more than half of all adult men and a third of all women belonged to clubs of various kinds' – there being 'more than 4,000 active associations' in Birmingham alone, 70 working-men's clubs in just Huddersfield (which also hosted 33 crown green bowling clubs), and more than 100 clubs/societies even in a 1960s new town such as Cumbernauld or similarly around 500 in Milton Keynes. And the 1970s was a decade 'in which membership of the Cubs, Brownies, Scouts and Guides reached record levels' (p 351).

Let us now leave the History of Our Clubs at c1990 and save for the Conclusion the issue of whether they are still, supposedly, a venue for the gatherings of 'the Establishment' in terms of whatever role(s) they fulfil in the new century and in the political world of Prime Ministers such as Blair, Brown, Cameron, and May - as opposed to that of Attlee (a regular at the Oxford and Cambridge), Wilson (the Athenaeum), and Macmillan (a member of half-a-dozen Clubs).

Chapter II – The Club in Literature

The stately clubs of London, how complacently they stand...

Gordon, 'A Gentlemen's Club', 1988

Clubland as *the world of the British Empire, in which leisured London clubmen waged a peacetime Great Game of war against cads, crooks and beastly foreigners*

Usborne, 'Clubland Heroes', 1983

Black (2012) provides an interesting and detailed analysis of the way the Clubs feature in such novels as: Trollope's *Phineas Finn* (1869); Disraeli's *Sybil* (1845); Thackeray's *Pendennis* (1848-50) and his 'Club Snobs' within the *Book of Snobs* (c1848); in *Punch* over the decades; in Galsworthy's *Forsyte Saga* (1922); in Wilde's *The Picture of Dorian Gray* (1890 - where 'the chatter of the clubs' helps bring Dorian down); in Robert Louis Stevenson's *The Suicide Club* (1878); and in Mark Lemon's 1850's farce *The Ladies' Club* which 'pits unhappy suspicious wives against their club-going husbands' with the lonely wives chorus trilling their determination to discover 'the secrets of those odious clubs' and eventually the wives forming 'The Ladies' Club' (*Punch* over the decades duly picked up on the scary idea of female clubbing and what the Victorians came to call the rise of 'femine clubland', running the cartoon 'Husbands in Waiting' with a bunch of forlorn chaps squatting outside the palatial premises as the clubhouse of The Ladies's Circle) .

BUCHAN (John), *The Thirty-Nine Steps* (1915). The novel begins with its gentleman-adventurer hero, Richard Hannay, bored and idle in London: '...on my way home I turned into my club - rather a pothouse, which took in Colonial members. I had a long drink, and read the evening papers'. Similarly, his *Greenmantle* (1916): the hero (again Major Hannay) narrates that 'I got a taxi and drove to my club... I went into the little back smoking-room, borrowed an atlas from the library, poked up the fire and sat down to think...' (and so the adventure begins).

CARTER (M.J.), *The Devil's Feast* (2016). 'The Reform Club was a political club, an alliance of Whigs and Radicals, or 'Liberals'... Opened for not quite a year in grand new premises in Pall Mall, it had quickly become the most desirable dining-room in London... [Pall Mall was] a series of edifices that would not have disgraced the Roman forum, temples to the interests and pursuits of the English gentleman... [The Athenaeum whose] members like to give themselves intellectual and philosophical airs... The club is invariably full of slumbering bishops. Far less interesting than it thinks it is... [The Reform] cost three times more than any other club on this street... [On Club Committees are to be found] ingrates who wish to be in charge over all things... The committee versus the members. The committee versus the kitchen... a thousand feuds and rivalries lurk...'

CARTER (Stephen), *New England White* (2007). Features the American Black community and its alleged secretive, networking, power-broking 'Establishment' clubs, here the 'Empyreals' (and, for women, the 'Ladybugs') – the former powerful enough supposedly to get its fixer installed as President 'of the country's most prestigious university'.

CHILDERS (Erskine), *The Riddle of the Sands* (1903). Again, as for the Buchan novels above, this novel begins with another bachelor gentleman, Carruthers, also bored in London and in need of adventure: '…a young man of condition and fashion, who knows the right people, belongs to the right clubs, has a safe, possibly a brilliant, future in the Foreign Office… had settled into the dismal but dignified routine of office, club, and chambers'. It is September and his usual Clubs are closed: 'Of course the club was a strange one, both of my own being closed for cleaning, a coincidence expressly planned by Providence for my inconvenience. The club which you are 'permitted to make use of' on these occasions always irritates with its strangeness and discomfort. The few occupants seem odd and oddly dressed, and you wonder how they got there. The particular weekly that you want is not taken in, the dinner is execrable, and the ventilation a farce. All these evils oppressed me tonight.'. Fortunately his old Oxford chum, Davies, proposes a sailing trip in the North Sea…

In modern spy novels, as a century ago with Buchan and Childers above, various suave characters are also to be found lunching, dining, and drinking at their Clubs in Pall Mall or St James's: for instance, in Robert Goddard's 'The Wide World' trilogy, in Len Deighton's 'London Match', and in Frederick Forsyth's 'Icon'. The Club is thus used as a short-hand for atmosphere, and often for 'the Establishment'; while membership thereof signals that the character has style and sophistication. Indeed, Gordon Corera in *The Art of Betrayal: Life and Death in the British Secret Service* (2011) comments: 'MI6 has slowly evolved from a self-selecting and self-perpetuating gentlemen's club for members of the establishment with a naughty streak to something more like a professional, bureaucratic organisation.'. Also in his *The Secret World: Behind the Curtain of British Intelligence in World War II and the Cold War* (2014) Hugh Trevor-Roper notes that the only ways into the Secret Service were via patronage or accident, and that he came into it by way of the latter since he did not belong 'to London clubland'. In *Tinker, Tailor* the top civil servants and the Circus heads are often to be found meeting up in their various Clubs. Christopher Andrew's 'authorised history of MI5' (*In Defence of the Realm*), however, in over 1000 pages makes no mention of Our Clubs being a source of recruitment or a venue for treacherous intrigue, but it does provide an amusing MI5 recruitment poster dispelling the myth that MI5 is 'like a gentlemen's club'. Usborne's *Clubland Heroes: A nostalgic study of some recent characters in the romantic fiction of Dornford Yates, John Buchan, and Sapper* (1983) comments that the Club was 'a convenient place for authors to put their heroes' – Buchan's Hannay; Yates' Berry; Sapper's Bulldog Drummond (and his enemy Carl Peterson with 'a taste in cigars and brandy' and 'a habit of expecting servants to look after him at the lifting of a finger'), as well as his Robert Standish as 'the games-playing clubman who solves problems of detection' and his Jim Maitland ('though his luggage may be in his London club, his heart is east of Suez'; he is 'the clubland hero whose luggage gathers dust for years under some sweeping staircase in Pall Mall or St James's').

CLEMENTS (Rory), *Corpus* (2017). The Establishment is active in 1936 London, as three 'important men in the life of the nation' (whose 'families had been close for generations' and who 'had been at prep school together, then Eton – same house – and Cambridge') are 'meeting over a decanter of brandy' in 'one of London's premier gentlemen's clubs' besides a blazing fire 'in the quietest corner, by one of the tall, curtained windows looking out over Pall Mall'. Later in the novel, as the Establishment plot thickens (fuelled by more brandy), 'the Foreign Office mandarin' of the trio 'swirled the brandy as he held it up to the light streaming in through the tall windows of the club's long room' and talks of 'a very convenient Russian agent' who has popped up in Cambridge (where else!).

COOPER (William) features Our Clubs in his series of novels: *Scenes from Metropolitan Life* (1982) re 1940s London, and *Scenes from Married Life* (1961) re London in c1950.

COX (Michael), *The Meaning of Night – A Confession* (2006). 'The establishment [a high-class Victorian brothel]... was known to the cognoscenti simply as 'The Academy', the definite article proclaiming that it was set apart from all other rival establishments, and alluding proudly to the superiority of its inmates, as well as to the services they offered. It was run along the lines of a highly select club – a Boodle's or a White's of the flesh – and catered for the amorous needs of the most discerning patrons of means. Like its counterparts in St James's, it had strict rules on admission and behaviour... blackballing was not infrequent...' (p 19).

DICKENS (Charles), *The Uncommercial Traveller* (1860s). 'Gentlemen's clubs were once maintained for purposes of savage party warfare... [but have become] places of quiet inoffensive recreation... [Similarly 'working men's clubs' in which] assuredly no one was louder than any at my club in Pall-Mall... I dined at my club in Pall-Mall aforesaid, a few days afterwards, for exactly twelve times the money, and not half as well.' (his essay XXV, 'The Boiled Beef of New England').

DISRAELI (Benjamin), *Endymion* (1881). Endymion tells St Barbe he lives in the Albany, his companion responding 'with an amazed and perturbed expression', and Endymion adding: 'I knew I could not be a knight of the garter, or a member of White's – the only two things an Englishman cannot command; but I did think I might some day live in the Albany.'. Endymion is based on Sir Charles Dilke and St Barbe on Thackeray, the latter character being an 'egotistical envious radical writer' and hence a rather unfair and 'grotesque' parody of Thackeray who had offended Disraeli almost twenty years earlier with his own parody of Disraeli in *Punch* (Blake, 1966, pp 733-739). Endymion also advises St Barbe that he should belong to a club; the latter responds that somebody else had suggested the Athenaeum, adding 'They rejected me and selected a bishop.' (Thackeray had in fact been black-balled for the Athenaeum in 1850, but then got in a year later.) . On Disraeli's death in 1881 'blinds were drawn over the windows of the great London clubs' (Blake, 1966, p 750).

DOYLE (Arthur Conan) has the Diogenes Club (Pall Mall) co-founded by Sherlock's brother, Mycroft Holmes, and the Club then appears in various of the original tales and also in the numerous TV versions of them; the most recent TV series 'Sherlock' (BBC), based on the Watson-Sherlock model but set in modern times, features the Diogenes Club so far in two episodes. In 'The Greek Interpreter' (within 'The Memoirs of Sherlock Holmes', 1894) Doyle introduces Mycroft and has Sherlock describe the Diogenes Club thus: 'The Diogenes Club is the queerest club in London, and Mycroft one of the queerest men... There are many men in London, you know, who, some from shyness, some from misanthropy, have no wish for the company of their fellows. Yet they are not averse to comfortable chairs and the latest periodicals. It is for the convenience of these that the Diogenes Club was started, and it now contains the most unsociable and unclubbable men in town. No member is permitted to take the least notice of any other one. Save in the Strangers' Room, no talking is, under any circumstances, allowed... My brother was one of the founders...'. See also the Horowitz entry below.

EDWARDS (Ruth Dudley), *Clubbed to Death* (1992); and also referred to in the next Chapter. Clubs, like Oxbridge colleges, do not have name-plates on their doors: '...the principle is that if a chap doesn't know where a club is, he shouldn't be allowed into it.' The Athenaeum is 'crammed full of bishops'; the Reform has 'too many economists, civil servants and PR men'; the Travellers is all 'wall-to-wall Foreign Office'; and 'the turnover in staff at ffeatherstonehaugh's [pronounced Fanshaw's] is spectacularly high even by club standards. They treat them badly and the inmates are madder than the norm...'. Two members of the Fanshaw's Committee ('a nest of greedy, self-centred, corrupt old men, of whom at least one would stick at nothing to preserve his privileges') do away with the reforming Chairman and also the new-broom Club Secretary lest they disturb the nefarious practices of theft and cocaine snorting... In *Publish and Be Murdered* (1999) - 'That's the trouble with institutions: they tend to take themselves seriously. Doesn't matter if it's parliament or the Jockey Club or Oxbridge colleges or gentlemen's clubs: they're all prone to be pompous and given to flummery...'

GILLESPIE (Harry), *The London Club* (2008). Victor Paulson, a dodgy businessman, ends up dead... 'As far as Paulson was concerned the fact that he was a member of the London Club was just as good as being a Lord of the British Isles.'

GORDON (Richard), *A Gentlemen's Club* (1988). Gordon is the author of the 'Doctor in the House' series, and he dedicates this book to 'My Fellow Clubmen'. He gives us the fictional 'The Albany', where the kitchens have just been inspected and promptly closed as unhygienic; its motto is 'Convivium Cum Cerebrum'; its crest is 'a Loaf of Bread, a Flask of Wine and a Book of Verse'; he comments that 'A club is the sum of its cliques'; and pokes fun at Club menus, 'Monday was Irish stew day' and the Committee always 'met on steak and kidney day'.

GREENE (Graham), *The Human Factor* (1978). The two characters, Dr Percival and Sir John Hargreaves, who had 'made a [monthly] habit of lunching alternatively at the Reform and the Travellers [as their respective Clubs]…', have discussed the relative merits of steak-and-kidney pudding versus its pie version and also Percival's uneasy conscience about having signed 'a declaration in favour of the Reform Act of 1886' upon becoming a Member of the Reform when he now rather felt it had 'opened the gates to the pernicious doctrine of one man one vote', walk 'down the great Gladstone stairs out into the chill of Pall Mall'.

GROSSMITH – see Chapter I re Pooter.

HARRIS (Robert), *Munich* (2017). Our strolling hero is a Foreign Office assistant secretary and 'all along Pall Mall, behind the tall windows of the great London clubs – the Royal Automobile, the Reform, the Athenaeum – the chandeliers glittered in the humid gloom'; but he has occasion to enter No. 10, 'as if he were entering some gentlemen's club that was no longer fashionable' with its 'grandfather clock ticking its leisurely heartbeat, the cast-iron umbrella stand with its solitary black umbrella' (perhaps Chamberlain's, for it is 1939) – although, as he ascended No. 10's main staircase 'the house had metamorphosed from gentlemen's club into a grand country mansion'. Deeper into the tale he 'had spent the night at his club' – where he 'had arrived to discover a backgammon evening in progress. Much strong drink had been taken. Until long after midnight the muffled noises of heavy male conversation and stupid laughter permeated the floorboards of his room…'. Over in Munich as he dodges the German watchers, he passes the entrance to some Turkish baths: 'A moist aroma of steam and sweet oils briefly released memories of the gentlemen's clubs of Pall Mall…'.

HOLT (Anthony), *Four of Clubs: Stories from the London Club World* (2014). Holt appears to have been a former Club Secretary of two Clubs and here he provides a collection of tales 'set in London's Clubland', some seemingly based on real events and characters – often frauds (the 'overbearingly unbearable' pompous but bogus 'Colonel', the fake 'Countess', the thieving 'Committee Man') . There is also 'Barbara', the Club employee, passing off her bottles of cheap plonk as the Club Claret and thereby building up a useful pension fund until caught (but the plonk is never detected by the members, duly distracted and well-satisfied by her liberal recharging of their glasses).

HOROWITZ (Anthony), *The House of Silk* (2011), 'The New Sherlock Holmes Novel'. As in the Doyle originals Mycroft Holmes is a member of 'The Diogenes Club in Pall Mall': 'Nobody ever spoke to each other. In fact, talking was not allowed at all, except in the Stranger's Room, and even there the conversation hardly flowed… the hall porter [*]had once wished a member good evening and had promptly been dismissed. The dining room had all the warmth and conviviality of a Trappist monastery, although the food was at least superior as the club employed a French chef of some renown... The Diogenes was one of the smaller clubs on Pall Mall, designed rather like a Venetian palazzo in the Gothic style... Visitors were permitted only on the ground floor... Mycroft received us, as always, in the Stranger's [sic] Room, with its oak bookshelves bowing under the weight of so many books, its various marble busts, its bow window with views across Pall Mall. There was a portrait of the Queen above the fireplace, painted, it was said, by a member of the club who had insulted her by including a stray dog and a potato, although I was never able to grasp the significance of either.' (pp 155-8).

[*] Girtin (1964, p 188) describes the typical Club Hall Porter: 'A Cerebus guarding the exclusiveness of the premises from unauthorized entry, with a memory for faces equalled only by the porter of an Oxbridge college, protecting the inmates against invasions of their privacy or violations of the sanctuary they had gained.'.

HULL (Richard) *Keep It Quiet* (1935). Benson, 'the best cook in Club-land', accidentally poisons a diner at the Whitehall Club; the Club Secretary, 'an amiable weak incompetent man', tries to hush things up. Hull comments: 'There is no more popular target for abuse than the committee of a club. ' (see the next Chapter on the role of the Club Committee).

'A LOUNGER AT THE CLUBS', *The Gentlemen's Art of Dressing with Economy* (1876). The guidance is for various kinds of decent chaps, including 'Club men': '... let us have a stroll in Clubland, where we shall see some of the best-dressed men, if not in Europe, at least in England... in the world of Clubland you find concentrated a

The Club in Literature

set of men of some social position... Along Pall Mall we walk, and observe those going in and out of its palatial halls. First we pass the OLD MAN CLUB [an 'asylum' for those 'in the evening of life' but still dressed with 'neatness and precision']... THE MINERVA CLUB [a distinctly scruffy set, the members being 'too deeply engrossed with Greek roots, fossil remains, and Professor Huxley's theories']... THE VOYAGERS adjacent is also of that ilk... REFORM in Tailors' Bills [has a few 'well-dressed men within its walls']... the stately TORY CLUB and its younger brother opposite – THE JUNIOR TORY [more interested in politicking than in 'any organized attempt to impart to the world of fashion']... THE OXBRIDGE AND CAMFORD ['teems with the parson element' where 'shovel hats and aprons abound']... and at the well-known RAG may be seen the best-dressed men all round in town [the haunt of the military officers]... NOODLE's ['dressed in the style fashionable fifty years ago']... It is easier to keep one's temper than one's umbrella... [Hence a useful tip:] At clubs an excellent plan prevails of placing one glove on top of the umbrella handle in the rack, retaining the other in your possession on the principle of the counterfoil in a blank cheque. A man must be mentally and morally abstracted to appropriate under these circumstances both glove and umbrella as his own; and if you detect one in the act, you will be justified in saying to him as Wellington did to Huskisson, 'It is no mistake, it can be no mistake, and it shall be no mistake.'.

Still thinking of umbrellas as of such concern in the book listed above, we take the next item out of alphabetical order...

WINTLE (Alfred) *The Club* (1961). The 1950s eccentric, Col. Wintle, dealt with this seemingly intractable problem of keeping one's umbrella secure in Clubland by leaving a Note in his permanently furled brolly ('This umbrella was stolen from Col. A.D.

Wintle'). Since, however, he also was known to have declared that 'No true gentleman would ever unfurl one', it is unclear how this tactic could work: the gentleman accidentally making off with Wintle's umbrella would anyway never unfurl it to discover the Note, while the bounder would open it at the first hint of rain and just keep the Wintle brolly, caddishly ignoring his Note. Wintle rightly features in 'Eccentric London' (Tom Quinn, 2005, p 31): inter alia, he was imprisoned for kidnapping the solicitor he accused of cheating his sister out of a legacy, but later won a civil action against the cad.

And yet another Clubland umbrella story: a notice on the board at the Carlton Club requested 'the nobleman who took an umbrella from the cloak-room' to return it; the notice-writer adding 'this is a club for noblemen and gentlemen, but, as no gentleman would take another's umbrella, so I am driven to the conclusion that the culprit must be a nobleman' (Girtin, 1964, p 87). At the O&C or the Athenaeum it could, of course, have easily been a bishop...

LYNN (Jonathan) & JAY (Anthony), *Yes Prime Minister* (1986, 1987). Volume I (p 246): 'Sir Humphrey met Sir Arnold for a drink that very evening at the Athenaeum Club. Sir Arnold's private diary relates what happened in full detail... 'Met a flustered and anxious Appleby at the club. After one brandy he revealed the cause of his panic. Apparently the Prime Minister and Geoffrey Hastings of MI5 both think he might be a spy, because he cleared Halstead and now Halstead has confessed all... Humphrey advanced several compelling arguments in his own favour... He was not at Cambridge... He is one of us... Unlike John Halstead, he has never believed in anything in his life... He, unlike Halstead, has never had any ideas – especially original ideas... These arguments are all persuasive – but not conclusive.'. Volume II (p 234): '... a meeting with Sir Arnold Robinson, his predecessor as Secretary of the Cabinet, at their old haunt, the Athenaeum Club...'. In the *Yes Minster* pre-cursor book these top Establishment civil servants also meet for lunch, drinks, dinner at their Club.

MUIR (Frank) *The Walpole Orange* (1994). 'William Grundwick has a problem. As secretary of the Walpole Club, he's duty bound to arrange whatever function the Events Committee decides is appropriate to celebrate the Club's 250th birthday. It's just that what they have decided upon seems to William almost wholly inappropriate...'

PEARS (Iain), *Stone's Fall* (2009). 'For those who have forgotten what London was like before the [1914-18] war, or who never knew, the very idea of an Anarchist Club sounds absurd. Most people are more familiar with the Reform, or the Athenaeum, and when they think of clubs, they think of leather armchairs, port and cigars, with quiet waiters padding about bearing silver platters. The idea of anarchists enjoying such surroundings cannot help bring a smile to the lips. Yet there was such a club [in the East End]...'

SAYERS (Dorothy L.), *The Unpleasantness at the Bellona Club* (1928). General Fentimen is found dead in 'a great chair' by 'the huge fireplace' in 'the spacious smoking-room' of the Bellona: the 'scandalised Bellonians' stagger to 'their gouty feet'. There is an incompetent Club Secretary, Captain Culyer, with a gammy arm; there is grumbling among the members about the Club Committee; and 'There never was anybody in the library'. Sayers' gentleman-amateur detective, Lord Peter Wimsey, is a member of the Marlborough Club and of the Egotists Club, is Eton and Balliol, and has a London address at 110A Piccadilly.

SCHOTT (Ben), *Jeeves and the King of Clubs* (2018). Featuring 'the private clubs of St James's', this homage to Wodehouse has Jeeves, long connected to MI5 as a member of the Junior Ganymede Club for domestic servants sharing intelligence-gathering activity, calling in help to deal with treason 'in the highest social circles' – help from Bertie Wooster! A mythical club is dissolved just to get rid of an awkward member ('He was preening, pedantic, and a thundering bore.'), who is then not admitted to the new club instantly formed – and this really happened in 1824 in the case of the Stratford Club faced with the troublesome Major General Thomas Charretie, dissolved and immediately reformed (sans Charretie) as the Portland Club. Bertie finds the Drones closed for refurbishment and that he is banished to the reciprocal club – the Athenaeum as 'the Club of Last Resort'…

STEWART (J.I.M. - aka 'Michael Innes' for his crime novels), *A Memorial Service* (1976). 'The Provost has given my father lunch at the Athenaeum.' 'Do you mean THE Athenaeum?' 'That's right – a club. Or not exactly a real club. Not like Boodle's or Buck's. A place for bishops and people of that sort.' 'Quite so.'

THACKERAY (William Makepeace), *The Book of Snobs* (1848), Chapters XXXVII-XLIV, 'Club Snobs' I-VIII. '… those social institutions, those palaces swaggering in St James's… [full of 'selfish' bachelors - young, middle-aged, old – whiling away time at] their present nightly orgies at the horrid Club [rather than leading domesticated married lives, some in] that den of abomination ['the Smoking Room']… The only men who, as I opine, ought to be allowed the use of Clubs, are married men without a profession…

The Club in Literature

[so as mercifully to be able to escape from a house of teenage daughters practising their musical instruments or being safely parked in the Club while the wife 'has a fancy to go to the milliners'!]... This sort of husbands should be sent out after breakfast... should be put into their Clubs, and told to remain there until dinner-time... Whenever I pass by St James's Street, having the privilege like the rest of the world, of looking in at the windows of 'Blight's', or of 'Foodles's', or 'Snook's', or the great bay at the 'Contemplative Club', I behold with respectful appreciation the figures within - the honest rosy old fogies, the mouldy old dandies, the waist-belts and glossy wigs and tight cravats of those most vacuous and respectable men. Such men are best there during the day-time surely... I belong to many Clubs, The 'Union Jack', the 'Sash and Marlin-Spike' – Military Clubs. 'The True Blue', the 'No Surrender', the 'Bluff and Buff', the 'Guy Fawkes', and the 'Cato Street – Political Clubs. 'The Brummel' and the 'Regent' – Dandy Clubs. The 'Acropolis', the 'Palladium', the 'Areopagus', the 'Pnyx', the 'Penticelicus', the 'Ilissus', and the 'Poluphloisboio Thalasses' – Literary Clubs. I never could make out how the latter set of Clubs got their names; I don't know Greek for one, and I wonder how many other members of those institutions do?... Why does not some great author write 'The Mysteries of the Club-houses; or St James's Street unveiled'?... I have remarked this excessive wine-amateurship especially in youth. Snoblings from college, Fledglings from the army, Goslings from the public schools, who ornament our Clubs, are frequently to be heard in great force upon wine questions. 'This bottle's corked,' says Snobling; and Mr Sly, the butler, taking it away, returns presently with the same wine in another jug, which the young amateur pronounces excellent... Club waiters, the civilist, the kindest, the patientist of men, die under the infliction of these cruel young topers...' (WMT himself belonged to the Garrick, the Athenaeum, and the Reform.)

In D.J. Taylor, 'The New Book of Snobs' (2016), we are informed that 'snobbery exists in all walks of life, at all social levels... at the checkout at Aldi as in a moated grange or the library of a Pall Mall gentlemen's club'. And later: 'a club snob who values a well-stocked cellar above human companionship'. Otherwise, however, Taylor compared to Thackeray lets Our Clubs off lightly.

TROLLOPE (Anthony), *The Warden* (1855). On the power of an article in the 'Jupiter' ('The Times'): 'Some great man, some mighty peer – we'll say a noble duke – retires to rest feared and honoured by all his countrymen – fearless himself... He rises in the morning, degraded, mean, and miserable; an object of men's scorn... What has made this awful change?... An article has appeared in the Jupiter... No man knows who wrote the bitter words; the clubs talk confusedly of the matter, whispering to each other this and that name; while Tom Towers [the Jupiter journalist] walks quietly along Pall Mall, with his coat buttoned against the east wind, as though he were a mortal man, and not a god dispensing thunderbolts from Mount Olympus [the Jupiter HQ].'.

Next *Barchester Towers* (1857). The country-bumpkin Squire Thorne has his Club membership for when in Town: 'When living at home at Ullathorne... he always looked like a gentleman, and like that which he certainly was, the first man in his parish. But during the month or six weeks he annually spent in London, he tried so hard to look like a great man there also, which he certainly was not, that he was put down as a fool by many at his club.' (Chapter XXII, 'The Thornes of Ullathorne').

And *The Small House at Allington* (1862), Chapter XXV: 'Adolphus Crosbie Spends an Evening at His Club'. 'He changed his clothes at his lodgings in Mount Street and went down to his club to dinner... as he entered the dinner room he saw one of his oldest and most intimate friends standing before the fire…'. Later they go 'up into the smoking-room', where then 'one of the club servants' comes in to tell Crosbie that a visitor was 'in the waiting room' (aka 'the stranger's [sic] room') who knows he is 'in the house', but to avoid a 'row in the house' Crosbie slips away 'down [Pall Mall?] to the Beaufort', another club.

Next, *The Way We Live Now* (1875), Chapter III on 'The Beargarden'. This is a Club for young rakes such as Sir Felix Carberry, and was probably based on the Marlborough Club (1869) as a sign of the decadent times Trollope was seeking to portray in this novel: 'Clubs were ruined, so said certain young parsimonious profligates, by providing comforts for old fogies who paid little or nothing but their subscriptions, and took out by their presence three times as much as they gave.' (hence The Beargarden did not open until 3pm and needed no morning-room in which to digest the free morning papers, nor a Library in which to snooze after such arduous endeavours).

Finally, *The Prime Minister* (1876). 'On that same day Lopez dined with his friend Everett Wharton at a new club called the Progress, of which they were both members. The Progress was certainly a new club, having as yet been open hardly more than three years; but still it was old enough to have seen many of the hopes of its early youth become dim with age and inaction. For the Progress had intended to do great things for the Liberal party – or rather for political liberality in general – and had in truth done little or nothing… The club, nevertheless, went on its way, like other clubs, and men dined and smoked and played billiards and pretended to read… the members generally, they were content to eat and drink and play billiards… [Lopez] had been heard to assert that, for real quiet comfort, there was not a club in London equal to it; but his hearers were not aware that in past days he had been blackballed at the T******* and the

G*******. These were accidents which Lopez had a gift of keeping in the background.' (Vol 1, Ch II). Later (Vol II, Ch LX) Lopez 'did go down to the Progress. The committee which was to be held with a view of judging whether he was or was not a proper person to remain a member of that assemblage had not yet been held, and there was nothing to impede his entrance to the club, or the execution of the command which he gave for tea and buttered toast. But no one spoke to him… Among members of the club there was a much divided opinion whether he should be expelled or not… [After all, one member, 'who was supposed to know the club-world very thoroughly', asked] 'If you turn out all the blackguards and all the dishonourable men, where will the club be?'… He drank his tea and ate his toast and read a magazine, striving to look as comfortable and as much at ease as men at their clubs generally are…' Spoiler alert! - He duly steps in front of 'the morning express down from Euston to Inverness' hurtling 'at a thousand miles an hour' though 'The Tenway Junction' and is 'knocked into bloody atoms'.

VERNE (Jules), *Around the World in 80 Days* (1873). Phileas Fogg is a wealthy bachelor member of the Reform Club, with rather fixed habits: 'The way in which he got admission to this exclusive club was simple enough. He was recommended by Barings [his upmarket bankers]'. He attends daily for breakfast and dinner (these meals being taken 'in the same room, at the same table'), leaving precisely at midnight; and the day on which he accepts the wager of £20,000 (today c£1.5m) begins normally enough: 'A flunkey handed him an uncut Times…'. Eighty days later he reappears as pledged to win the bet: 'At the fifty-seventh second the door of the saloon opened; and the pendulum had not beat the sixtieth second when Phileas Fogg appeared, followed by an excited crowd who had forced their way through the club doors…'

WOODEHOUSE (P.G.) invented the Drones Club (Dover Street, Mayfair) for the idle young men of his stories; probably based on the Arts Club, the Bachelors' Club, Buck's, and the Bath Club – the Drones bartender, McGarry, being named after the Buck's barman who created or popularised Buck's Fizz. Here are just a couple of instances of the Club featuring in a tale: 'Now, one advantage of having a row with a girl in Bruton Street is that the Drones is only just around the corner, so that you can pop in and restore the old nervous system with the minimum of trouble.' – and certainly no risk of said girl following you in to continue the difficult conversation! ('The Amazing Hat Mystery'). And from Chapter 4 of 'Uncle Fred in the Springtime': 'The atmosphere in the smoking-room of the Drones Club on the return of its members from their annual week-end at Le Touguet was not always one of cheerfulness and gaiety [given the danger of gambling losses, but this year the 'dingy gods' of the 'Continental Casinos' had] been extraordinarily kind to many of Eggs, Beans and Crumpets revelling in the bar.'. In another tale the Drones are relocated to 'the Senior Liberal' while their Club-house is given 'a wash and brush-up'; the Senior Liberal does not appeal: 'I mean, when you've got used to a club where everything's nice and cheery, and where, if you want to attract a fellow's attention, you heave a bit of bread at him, it kind of damps you to come to a place where the youngest member is about eighty-seven, and it isn't considered good form to talk to anyone unless you and he went through the Peninsular War together.'.

ZAFON (Carlos Ruiz), *The Labyrinth of the Spirits* (2017). In Barcelona a 'lavish fossil' of a former family palace has become the Equestrian Club as 'one of those unassailable and elegant institutions left to ferment in all great cities' – where 'humans strive for reasons to feel superior to others, and resources with which to demonstrate that superiority. The club seemed to have been fashioned for that very end…'. It was a place for 'self-appointed elites' – 'And the brandy is superb'.

And the Clubs and Clubland on film and the TV?

In 'Yes Minister' and 'Yes Prime Minister' – see Lynn & Jay above, and Chapter I.

In Fleming's 'Moonraker' where Bond dines with M at Blades – see Chapter I.

In 'I'm All Right Jack', an Ealing comedy – see Chapter I.

In 'Bootsie and Snudge', a 1960s' TV sitcom – see Appendices, Clubs Fictional; and also (*) below…

In 'Around the World in 80 Days' – see above under Verne: has been on the stage in several versions, on the radio, and in film (as early as 1919, but famously starring David Niven in 1956, and most recently in 2004 starring Steve Coogan); also as a board game and on TV. The Reform Club is usually portrayed.

In the BBC Radio 4 series, 'The Small, Intricate Life of Gerald C. Potter', Gerald gets anxious that his wife is becoming a 'club-woman' by joining a Ladies' Club (Series 2, Episode 3) .

The 'Fun Library' provided 'Society and Clubland' (edited by Hammerton) which offers many illustrations of Club life; and also similarly 'Mr Punch in Society' as another volume in the 'Fun Library'. See also Cohn-Sherbok (2018) for a collection of 'sketches' of London Clubland faces.

Finally, a 2017 production of *Die Meistersinger* at Covent garden staged it in what some reviewers (including BBC2's 'Newsnight') saw as a male-only London club, the production being interpreted as a rant against institutionalised, establishment, old boys Britain from the Danish director, Kasper Holten: German reviews detected elite *Herrenclubs*. Other reviews, however, perceived the setting as, variously, a London livery hall with the Meistersingers as pompous liverymen in full regalia or as a Freemasons' Hall with the Meistersingers in masonic bibs – the livery 'movement' and freemasonry are often confused and assumed to share common medieval origins (they do not – Palfreyman, 2010).

(*) Such is the author's donnish commitment to the toil of research that some of the thirty-nine episodes of Series 1 of 'Bootsie and Snudge' (as dimly remembered from his black & white TV childhood) have been viewed (Series 1 from 1960 to 1963 and also Series 2 in 1974 available on DVD), and the following duly noted:

- It is a spin-off from Granada's 'The Army Game' putting National Servicemen Bootsie (Alfie Bass) and his bullying sergeant Snudge (Bill Fraser) into Civvy Street as, respectively, the dogsbody and Hall Porter staff of 'The Imperial Club' along with Clive Dunn as the decrepit bumbling barman 'Old Johnson' and Robert Dorning as the pompous Club Secretary, the Rt Hon Hesketh Pendleton (aka 'The Rt Hon Sec'). The Series was written by Barry Took and Marty Feldman.

- The first half-dozen episodes of series one introduce the Club characters... Bootsie and Snudge hoping never to see each other again as they are being demobbed, the former resenting the latter's forever issuing orders when in the Army and the latter frustrated that he no longer has command over the former. They end up meeting again at the Labour Exchange and each get sent for a job at the 'Members Only' Imperial Club, the grandly (re-)uniformed Snudge as its Major Domo and Bootsie as the Bootboy and put-upon general dogsbody. Snudge is shown reciting the many Club Rules and saluting the Club Secretary, and also coping with the deaf and confused 'Old Johnson' who thinks Snudge is Lord Kitchener. They seek and get endless 1s tips from the gentlemen members despite the NO TIPPING sign; the Reading Room is full of snoozing elderly gents in club-chairs with newspapers over their heads; one member is the Head of MI5; Bootsie is supposed to be married in the Clubhouse to Rita the Kitchen-maid by a member who is the Chaplain of Wormwood Scrubs; the members have voted against having a TV-set in the Club – but get excited when Snudge acquires one and they can watch the football match; there is a member who is a Major with a monocle.
- All in all, the Club is being used as a setting in which to play out class distinctions and social aspiration (Snudge's strangulated vowels) in 1950s Britain; and with a little gentle mockery of the restrictiveness, conventions, and social hierarchy of post-War England and also of the disintegrating Empire.
- Sadly the Series has not worn well, in the way that the classic 'Dads Army' has from a few years later – but it clearly gave Clive Dunn the chance to practice as Old Johnson the similar role he subsequently played as Corporal Jones.

Chapter III – The Club in Law

A man thinks of his club as a living being, honourable as well as honest… [as located within] those luxurious club-houses in Pall Mall… [and as part of] the spirit of association…

Maitland

All its members remain jointly and severally liable for its actions done within their authority

The Court of Appeal, in 2008, re the criminal liability exposure of the entire cohort of 900 members of a golf club

Our Clubs are not companies as if Tesco or British Airways, and hence created and regulated under the Companies Act 2006. Nor are they chartered corporations as if Oxbridge Colleges or the Livery Companies (Palfreyman, 2010, Part Two: 'Law relating to the London Livery Companies'), and hence created by Royal Charter and regulated by the law of corporations. And they are not charities as if Oxfam or the Oxbridge colleges, and hence registered with the Charity Commission and regulated under the Charities Act 2011. They are akin to the Inns of Court (Palfreyman, 2011, Chapter V) in being, generally, unincorporated associations – as are, say, also the JCRs of Oxbridge colleges, the South Molton Bowling Club, the Bampton & Clanfield History Society, or the Oxford Management Club as a dining society. That said, Clubs may increasingly become incorporated so as to protect their managing committee and even the wider membership against personal financial liability – risks explained below...

Burrows (2007, paras 3.110-113) explains the concept of the unincorporated association: 'an unincorporated association comes into being whenever a group of associates creates an organisational system, from the existence of which the courts are prepared to infer that the associates intend to be legally bound to one another... the members' rights between themselves are [then] governed exclusively by the terms of the association's rules... So long as their common purpose is not illegal, the associates may combine to do anything they wish, be it the pursuit of personal pleasure or advantage [Our Clubs], or some other purpose... Unincorporated associations are not considered to be artificial persons under English law, but are seen as amorphous collections of individuals...'. The association's rules will probably require members to pay annual subscriptions. The association may hold property in one of several ways, but the usual form is for it to be held by all members subject to being contractually bound to each other only to use the property in accordance with the rules of the association – the members place the property for convenience in the hands of the association's officers as custodians. The members are not contractually liable for each other's acts or for those of the officers; the officers, if they have behaved properly, are likely to be indemnified from the association's funds if sued by a third-party, who might otherwise in theory sue all the members if the entire membership can be said to have agreed the action complained of; more commonly the litigation is a representative action against a named member or an officer. Given all this complexity, almost all sizeable economic activity is done by way of an artificial person – a company or a corporation, and indeed the Inns of Court as big businesses are very odd in being unincorporated associations.

The Club in Law

The legal concept of the association has attracted some fine minds, including F.W. Maitland (1850-1906), the Cambridge historian of English law, who, inter alia, studied the development of the corporation from Roman law and also of 'the trust idea' in English law - seeing the latter as 'the greatest and most distinctive achievement performed by Englishmen in the field of jurisprudence' and as 'the greatest feat that men of our race have performed in the field of jurisprudence'. There could be noble features related to this legal idea: 'A man thinks of his club as a living being, honourable as well as honest...' while the business partnership or the company is merely about money-making; and 'the spirit of association' is essential to democracy, something not to be controlled by the domineering Napoleonic State as across the Channel and something that engendered social or intellectual as well as political liberties. Maitland duly noted that 'every judge on the bench is a member of at least one club' and he cited the Jockey Club in addition to 'those luxurious club-houses in Pall Mall'. It was 'this world of associations' (as Alan Macfarlane explains in 'F.W. Maitland and the Making of the Modern World') – so familiar that 'it becomes invisible' - and of 'associationalism' as part of English and American life, of 'the power of associations', that fascinated Maitland as 'filling the teeming middle space of open, democratic societies' with entities that are 'the bane of all authoritarians': 'participation in such self-governing associations is the main bulwark against dictatorship', as 'a community of communities' that includes Our Clubs (which doubtless would have had to be 'snuffed out' in Roman Law States – as with the elimination of the guilds we still retain by way of the London Livery Companies inherited form the Middle Ages or of the university colleges which we still cherish as the medieval glories of the Oxford & Cambridge Colleges, as well as the similarly ancient Inns of Court).

Maitland considered the case of clubs in his essay on 'Trust and Corporation' (from which most of the quoted phrases in the above paragraph are drawn). He notes that 'the London tradesmen are willing enough to supply goods to clubs on a large scale' since the tradesman trusts the club even if, as he probably does not realise, he could not easily sue the unincorporated association as he might resort to suing a debtor company or perhaps a Bertie Wooster who had failed to pay his bills; this trust is unwittingly based partly on the fact that scandals over unpaid bills 'have been very rare' and partly because in the event of a debt 'the members of the club would in all probability treat the case as if it were one of corporate liability'. And all despite the fact that: 'The 'ownership in equity' that the member of the club has in land, buildings, furniture, books etc is of a very strange kind' – being founded in the idea that 'we have to suppose numerous tacit contracts which no one knows that he is making, for after every election there must be a fresh contract between the new member and all the old members. But every judge on the bench is a member of at least one club, and we know that if a thousand tacit contracts have to be discovered, a tolerable result will be attained.'

In 'Halsbury Laws of England' we find 'Clubs' divided into 'member's clubs' (such as Our Clubs) and 'propriety clubs' (founded, owned, and run by an individual as indeed were some of the eighteenth-century early versions of the Pall Mall and St James's clubs; and as also are a new breed of clubs spreading across London in recent decades and, although the idea of a pioneering individual, now in effect run as a limited company). In Halsbury clubs are defined as 'a society of persons associated together, not for the purposes of trade, but for social reasons, the promotion of politics, sport, art, science or literature, or for any other lawful purpose' (although trading within the club as 'merely incidental to the club's purposes' is fine). The members' club funds itself from one-off entrance fees and from its annual subscriptions; it is usually unincorporated and has no legal existence 'apart from the members of which it is composed'; the members own the assets in equal shares; they agree and apply a set of Rules. The usual laws concerning health & safety, food hygiene, licensing, the minimum wage, employment, planning, listed buildings, nuisance, corporation tax, VAT, PAYE, rates, etc, apply – although not the Data Protection Act 2008 in full. Some members' clubs may, however, be incorporated under the Companies Act 2006 and hence the club becomes itself a legal entity, and again there will be a set of Rules. A propriety club is owned by the individual (who may be a company) who is the proprietor running it for profit who then is in a contractual relationship with the member(s).

The members' club Rules are a contract among the members and cover matters such as the election and expulsion of members, the payment of fees and subscriptions, the club's management, the conduct of meetings of members, the structure of committees, the changing of the rules, the keeping of accounts, the opening hours, the admission of guests. All such Rules 'must be applied in accordance with the principles of natural justice' and are thereby subject to review in the Courts: an injunction can be sought 'to prohibit wrongful expulsion'. A member in default on the payment of the subscription can be expelled (assuming the Rules so provide) and be sued as a debtor. Any expulsion must carefully follow the process set out in the Rules: proper enquiry, due notice, chance for the member to be heard in his/her defence, the decision-makers acting in good faith and reasonably, and so on (the case of *Labouchere v Earl of Wharncliffe* (1879) 13 ChD 346 concerned expulsion from the Beefsteak Club). Where the expulsion procedure is defective, the Court can declare the expulsion invalid and order the club officers/employees to let the member in. The members are not liable for the club's debts, but the members of the managing committee may end up with personal liability. The assets of the club if it is wound up are divided equally among the current members (unless the Club Rules declare a different procedure will apply, and the Court intervening if necessary where whatever process is not being done properly – *Re St James's Club v Hastings* (1852) 2 De GM &G 383).

In the 1879 *Labouchere* case, L gained an injunction to prevent the Beefsteak Club expelling him; the Committee (represented in the action by the Earl of Wharncliffe, probably as its Chairman) had failed to follow proper procedure in deciding that L's behaviour was 'injurious to the welfare and interests of the club' under its Rule 20. Jessel MR (Master of the Rolls) expressed surprise that the Committee had managed so comprehensively to mess up the process when there had been 'such clear rules' and hence the Court duly found for L on every count of irregularity caused by the Committee's lack of 'good common sense' as 'a body of English gentlemen'. The Court's task was not to second-guess any decision reached by the Committee; it was not an appeal court. But its task was to review whether and ensure that the Committee had followed a proper and fair process in reaching a decision, including adhering to the published Club Rules about such matters as the length of notice given for a meeting and on voting at such a meeting.

The importance of the precise bureaucratic process of updating Club Rules was illustrated in *Harrington v Sendall* (1903) 1 Ch 921, as cited in *Wertheimer's Law Relating to Clubs* (1913, pp 20/21) as 'the Oxford and Cambridge Club case', where the Club had no rule authorising the making of new rules or the alteration of existing ones, so H (and others) gained the requested injunction preventing the Club increasing his annual subscription to £9.45 from £8.40: the 1885 Rules from the year H joined still applied in 1902 since the Club had forgotten to give itself power to update them and hence was unable to change the 1885 stated annual fee. The Wertheimer text has about a dozen Clubland cases, and a whole chapter on 'Expulsion' that runs to 50 pages within 170.

We get even more detailed treatment in Nicholas Stewart et al (2011, OUP), *The Law of Unincorporated Associations*, which opens with a Foreword: 'What does one's golf club or freemasons' lodge have in common with the Carlton Club and the local working men's club, the sewing circle, and model railway club? Or with the Oxford Union, the National Union of Seamen…? [The answer is that they] are unincorporated associations [where folk] are drawn together for purpose and to pursue common interests of all kinds… Such associations may be small or very large, local or national; they are both very numerous and astonishingly diverse… They do, however, give rise to difficult legal problems… the subject is of considerable complexity…' (Lord Millett). The Preface asks, if the club has no legal identity, who of the members will be 'responsible for the cost of beer supplied for the clubhouse?'. And, 'if a cleaner slips', who may be liable for his/her injury? Who might be prosecuted under the Health & safety at Work etc Act 1974? Plus: 'When can members challenge decisions of the executive committee? What rights of redress are available to an expelled member, and against whom?'. The text draws on some 600 relevant cases and lists well over 100 items of legislation applicable to these unincorporated associations 'unique to common law systems': from the Inns of Court (Palfreyman, 2011) to our humble Clubs. What more does this authoritative volume tell us about our Clubs beyond what has been set out above? (See also Smith (2008) on 'Club Law and Management for Private Membership Clubs'; 'Ashton and Reid on Club Law', 2010; and Barker & Stevens (2011), 'Club Law Manual'.)

Well, they are certainly not partnerships – as established in *Harrington v Sendall* [1903] 1 Ch 921 concerning the Oxford and

Cambridge University Club. Lawton LJ in the case of *Conservative and Unionist Central Office v Burrell (Inspector of Taxes)* [1982] 1 WLR 522 (CA) defined an unincorporated association as: 'two or more persons bound together for one or more common purposes, not being business purposes, by mutual undertakings, each having mutual duties and obligations, in an organisation which has rules which identify in whom control of it and its funds rests and upon what terms and which can be joined or left at will'. In *Hopkinson v Marquis of Exeter* (1867) LR 5 Eq 63 Lord Romilly MR recognised that Our Clubs are 'very peculiar institutions' and primarily social: hence it is 'necessary that there should be a good understanding between all the members, and that nothing should occur that is likely to disturb the good feeling that ought to subsist between them' (no cads and bounders, please!).

Applications for membership should be treated consistently (and 'with honesty, integrity, and fairness'), but there is no requirement to give reasons for a membership decision and the Courts will not intervene unless the process has been discriminatory or otherwise unlawful. (Indeed, as Ralph Waldo Emerson noted in his 1909 essay on 'Clubs', it is the case that 'the club must be self-protecting... always a practical difficulty to regulate the laws of election so as to exclude peremptorily every social nuisance' so as 'to secure liberal and refined conversation'.) It may be possible to raise additional funds in a financial emergency by imposing a levy on all members; conversely the Club can distribute any profits/surplus among its members (as indeed did the RAC when it sold off its interest in the RAC as a car-breakdown service, each member getting c£30k). Clubs can amalgamate to their mutual benefit, and many have over the centuries of Clubland's existence. The Club's management processes will be as in its Rules, subject to the general law of meetings and chairing thereof (notably *John v Rees* [1970] Ch 345

(Ch) – for example, the chair has a casting vote only if the Rules say so since in common law there is no such concept).

The Club's Rules must not contravene the Equality Act 2010 which applies to an 'association' defined in s107(2) EqA10 as 'an association of persons' having at least 25 members. Thus, the Club must not discriminate in respect of the protected characteristics (age, disability, gender reassignment, marriage or civil partnership, pregnancy and maternity, race, religion or belief, sex or sexual orientation) – but associations may restrict membership other than on the basis of race. In the case of disability there must be 'reasonable adjustments' to the premises – causing, as with the Oxbridge colleges, a potential conflict with gaining Listed Building Consent. A Club can indeed, lawfully, remain single-gender, but if it, say, begins to accept women members it would be unlawful to discriminate among the mixed membership be having a class of 'Lady Member'. A 'Junior Member' class based on not having reached a certain age is lawful, as is a class of 'Senior Member' on the basis of having reached a specified age – each category might pay reduced annual subs, as might members living in the Provinces rather than in London.

The holding of Club assets and property is generally under the 'contract-holding theory' involving a mixture of co-ownership and contract (following Cross J in *Neville Estates Ltd v Madden* [1962] Ch 832 (Ch D); and *Hanchett-Stamford v AG* [2009] Ch 173 (Ch) similarly): 'The current members will own the association's property as joint tenants but those members' rights under the joint tenancy will be subject to their mutual contract with each other on the terms of the rules.' (para 3.05 of Stewart et al, 2011). Only if the Club is dissolved can the then members get their individual share (if anything is left! – and it is anyway inconceivable that any of Our Clubs should ever fade away…). The lease of the land on which the

Clubhouse stands will usually be in the name of Club officers as tenants, the lease being reassigned as the officers change. Incorporation, of course, overcomes all these complexities.

The disciplining of members has to be in accordance with the Club's Rules (which in turn must comply with natural justice – *Young v Ladies' Imperial Club Limited* [1920] 2 KB 523 (CA) and similar cases such as *Labouchere* cited above), these being rules as signed up to by the member joining the Club and thereby entering into an assumed or implied mutual contract with all the other members. The usual reason to discipline a member is that 'a member's conduct is detrimental or injurious to the character or interests of the association'. The member has no right to be legally represented or to bring a lawyer to any such disciplinary hearing before a domestic tribunal convened under the Club Rules, but a friend should probably be allowed to accompany the member; the tribunal has no need to give reasons for its decision, unless specifically ordered by the Court; there is no automatic right of internal appeal, but a Club's Rules may set up an appeal mechanism. The Human Rights Act 1998 generally will not apply to the domestic disciplinary tribunals of unincorporated associations since they do not determine civil rights but merely private contractual rights arising from membership of the Club. The issue of expulsion becomes potentially even more fraught in the age of emails (Who is saying what to whom, when, and about whom?) and also in the context of social media (Will X launch off in cyber-space about the Club and how, if at all, can the Club then respond to defend itself?) .

In the 1920 *Young* case the Court of Appeal found that the executive committee of the Ladies' Imperial Club had not been properly convened: the Duchess of Abercorn had not been sent notice of the meeting, and it was no excuse for the Club to assert that the Duchess would anyway not have bothered to attend even if summoned; she should have been given the chance to attend, and so, declared the Court, 'this meeting is bad' as 'an invalid meeting' and 'not a proper committee'. Thus, 'there is some public importance in making clear to club committees that they must act regularly in the expulsion of members…': that is, they must follow set down procedures carefully. With luck, however, the Management Committee will not have to face an expelled member appearing in the Hall waving a sword, as at the Athenaeum in 1869 (Girtin, 1964, p 61).

In *Dawkins v Antrobus* (1881) 17 ChD 615 a member expelled from the Travellers Club brought a case in the Chancery Division asserting that there had been insufficient notice of the charge against him in the expulsion process: Brett LJ ruled that the principles of natural justice applied in that there had to be a fair hearing. (This case was cited in a High Court decision of 2016 concerning the rules of the Labour Party and who was eligible to vote in the election of Jeremy Corbyn as its Leader: [2016] EWHC 2058 (QB), Royal Courts of Justice.) Similarly, in *Fisher v Keane* (1879) 11 ChD 353 the Club Committee was obliged to act according to the principles of natural justice: here two members made 'a statement' on what Major Fisher was supposed to have 'said and did in the billiard room on the night in question' within the Army and Navy Club and the Committee simply acted upon that 'to blast a man's reputation for ever… without giving him an opportunity of either defending or palliating his conduct' (Jessel MR); the Court duly issued the injunction sought by the Major. Back to Colonel William Dawkins of the Travellers Club – he had earlier brought a case, indeed repeated actions, against the army officers who had been involved in his being deprived of his commission following a court-martial: the Court eventually lost patience with the litigious ex-Colonel and dismissed his claims as 'utterly hopeless' in *Dawkins v Prince Edward of Saxe Weimar* (1876) 1 QBD 499 (so, he had 'form' by the time he became a subsequently unwelcome member of the Travellers).

The member of a Club is not liable to the Club's creditors unless he/she personally was involved in incurring the debt (Lord St Leonards LC in *Re St James's Club* as above). The principals to a contract will usually be the members of the Executive or Management Committee, and hence the Club Rules need to be clear on who has precisely what authority to order exactly what from whom. The employment contracts are with the members of the Committee, although there is uncertainty as to whether the change of Committee members means the employment contract has to be constantly updated. The Committee members will probably be given within the Club Rules an indemnity for their properly-taken decisions, but, if not, there may well be an implied right of indemnity under certain circumstances – and the Club may anyway have directors and officers liability insurance cover. Similarly it will have in place other insurance policies to cover employer and public liability for staff or visitors injured in the Clubhouse, although a claim or a tort action will be brought against representative named members of the Committee and the claim/litigation will be handled by the insurer. Here, in the context of a hefty award in tort, the whole membership could in theory end up jointly and severally liable to meet the cost of any compensation or damages awarded where that cost might exceed the sums insured and the financial assets of the Club – the wealthiest member could be targeted to meet the entire shortfall, leaving him/her trying recover portions from all the other members! Again, this could be one factor in prompting incorporation – as might potential problems arising from under-funded pension schemes?

Thus, the injured cleaner claims and the insurer pays if there has been negligence; the member's drunk visitor falling down the stairs because of a loose carpet also sues and is compensated by the public liability cover; the same visitor falling over simply because he/she is so drunk has no claim (and perhaps should be banned!) unless the Club could be said to have been on notice from his/her past behaviour to limit access to the temptations of the Bar; and the two aggressively competitive squash-players injuring each other have no claim against the Club unless further injury was caused by defective squash-court flooring. If, however, one of the players is in fact a Club employee taking revenge upon an arrogant member then conceivably the Club could be vicariously liable as employer. The same might apply if a waiter frustrated by the persistent rudeness of an ignorant member tipped the soup tureen over his head - unless the Club could argue such was a frolic of the employee's own and nothing to do with the Coffee Room duties (that line of defence, however, is becoming increasingly difficult for employers).

But where the injured party is a member there is no liability for the Club (unless incorporated?) since there is 'no duty of care owed by the members to each other and accordingly no action can be brought in respect of injuries on club premises' (para 8.29 of Stewart et al, 2011). The Club Rules, presumably, do not expressly guarantee the safety of the Clubhouse and the Court will not imply such a term as a mutual commitment among the members. There could perhaps be an inadvertent assumption of a duty of care if, say, member X organises a Club activity for other members and should reasonably have foreseen that, say, kayaking in Iceland for the Club Table members of the Oxford and Cambridge might not be a good idea – although that spirited bunch equally could be said willingly to have assumed the risk when confronted by the exciting challenge of the icy rapids. The Athenaeum is probably liable in nuisance if it uses its little garden as a go-karting track for its members and distracts the adjacent Royal Society great-minds. The unincorporated Club is not able to sue for defamation; only its individual members. The defamatory statements in the Club News could leave the Committee or its Editor being sued, and libel proceedings may not be covered by any insurance the Club has while any indemnity within the Club Rules will not kick in if the defamation was recklessly or intentionally made.

There can be criminal liability for 'a body of persons corporate or incorporate' as a 'person' (Interpretation Act 1978), but who goes to prison if not the entire membership of the Diogenes Club? There can be prosecution of the entity, where a fine could be levied on the Club itself; but individual members could also be prosecuted (*R v RL and JF* [2008] EWCA Crim 1970 re pollution of a watercourse at a golf club from a leaky oil-tank, and one with 900 members), and people can go to prison – in theory, the entire membership of, say, the Athenaeum. The likelihood is that the Club Chair and/or key Committee members with relevant specific responsibilities would be singled out by the CPS – as indeed in the above case. But no personal individual fault would be required, simply that the Club is at fault – or it is a strict liability offence, as in *RL*. A leading textbook – *Smith & Hogan's Criminal Law* (14th edition, 2015, pp 303-306) comments that the decision in *RL* for the members of an unincorporated association is so astounding that it 'deserves parliamentary attention' – perhaps so that it can be legislated that the unincorporated association shall be treated akin to the process for determining the criminal liability of incorporated company officers, and not leaving the membership exposed in total. Of course, a Club chairperson would probably feel at home in an open-prison and might soon organise fellow prisoners, get the prison library tidied up, improve the cuisine (if not the cellar)…

Two final comments from Stewart et al (2011) reinforcing the message that should now be clear about the Club needing a competent Management Committee and an efficient Secretary, and that those Good Citizens taking on a management Committee stint needing to do so with eyes open: first, in relation to tort claims based on negligence leading to personal injury, 'In many cases the entire membership at the date of the accident will be exposed to liability as joint tortfeasors. Members who have nothing to do with the running of the club could still incur a substantial liability in tort if a guest is severely injured [usually cheaper to kill 'em straight off!] due to the defective state of the club premises.' (para 11.55); and, secondly, where there is litigation against representative members, 'Those named individuals must take special care to ensure that they do not accept the risk of being financially hung out to dry where it is the association's funds and the membership as a whole which ought to accept those risks.' (para 9.73).

On the importance of the Club Committee Nevill (1911) noted: 'An absolute essential to the prosperity of a club is a good committee...' (p 158) – albeit that: 'Committee-men, it should be added, whether good, bad, or indifferent, generally have a rather difficult task, for they are certain to arouse the opposition of some professional grumbler or other who is ever ready to blame.' (p 170). Darwin (1943) comments on 'wasted' words and hours in such committee meetings, musing that 'a club is often best managed by a dictator who knows his business and knows when and where to stop', ruling 'so tactfully that his subjects never dream that they are being ruled at all' (p 14) – so, much the same skill-set as required for the successful Head of House in an Oxbridge college? That said, however, for Nevill it is an 'efficient' Club Secretary 'who in reality runs most clubs' since 'the majority of house committees are [not] in any way zealous about carrying out their functions' (p 170). And, doubtless, this efficient paragon gets little or no thanks, just as also for the humble Clerk of a Livery Company or the down-trodden Bursar of an Oxford college. Girtin (1964), like Nevill (1911), stresses the need for a competent Secretary ('the qualities called for in a secretary are of a very special order', p 58) . The Travellers Club (founded 1819) is a good example of improved fortunes after gaining a more professional Club Secretary from the 1980s (Robinson, 2018).

Back in 1911 for Nevill (as seemingly then, now, and always) one of the 'wicked' issues in Clubland was getting rid of unwanted members, given the problem of quite defining just why they were deemed to be a nuisance: 'Members who have developed undue eccentricity occasionally cause uneasiness to their fellow-clubmen, for it is sometimes difficult exactly to define the point at which personal idiosyncrasies become disquieting to others.' (p 201). The boozy member so common in the eighteenth-century clubs seems by the Edwardian era to be distinctly frowned upon: 'A striking change in club-life is the vastly decreased consumption of alcohol… even the slightest tendency to habitual excess is seriously resented; a decided stigma, indeed, attaches to anyone even suspected of intemperance, while any demonstration of inebriety would certainly call forth demands for drastic measures being applied to the member indulging in such a breach of club law.' (pp 192/3) – except one assumes at the Drones Club frequented by Bertie Wooster! As a result, there had been 'the great decrease of club receipts derived from the sale of wine and spirits'. Conversely, Nevill (1911) comments on the increase in smoking over recent decades, something he welcomes by way of the relaxation of the former stringent 'out-of-date' and 'absurd' restrictions as a 'prejudice' – and anyway tobacco-smoke in the Club Library 'can have nothing but a beneficial effect upon books, which it has a tendency to preserve' (p 147). Griffiths (1907, p 210) refers to those among 'Club Habitues' (Chapter X) who are beyond being just a mere 'Rum Chap' and are 'more distinctly dotty', being 'palpably maniacs, men whose mental deficiencies amount to aberration of intellect and positive lunacy' –

even if the actually 'insane' only occasionally 'become really dangerous'!

A Club's 'Guide' for its members might tell them that the Club's property 'is held by Trustees appointed at the AGM which is held each June'. The same AGM elects 'The Committee' in order for it 'to manage the Club', meeting ten times a year; the Committee duly elects 'the Club's Chairman and Vice-Chairman' – it also 'appoints the Secretary who is in effect the Club's chief executive' and who is 'assisted by two Assistant Secretaries and a Financial Controller'. This well-run Club, let's say it is one of the larger ones in Clubland with some 3000 members and a turnover in excess of £4m, 'employs nearly 100 staff'. Its Committee has a number of Sub-Committees: Buildings and Fabric, Cards (sic), Catering and Services, Club Events, Election, Library, Management (aka Finance & General Purposes), Membership, Sports, Wine, and Younger Members. Membership of some Sub-Committees clearly sounds more fun than of others. Its AGM Agenda might typically deal with the Annual Report of the Committee, the Annual Accounts, and the election of Committee Members for the next year.

The Accounts of a Club will probably show Income from Subscriptions, Catering (Food and Drink), perhaps Bedroom Lettings if the Club has rooms, and Miscellaneous; while Expenditure will be on Staff, Buildings (rent if applicable, rates, insurance, utilities, maintenance, cleaning, etc), Administration (copying, postage, phones, IT, perhaps the Library if one, etc). The Club might hope the latter exceeds the former, any surplus being used for, say, the creation of a Maintenance Reserve, a General Reserve, and (if applicable) a Leasehold Sinking Reserve (to cover the periodic renewal of the leasehold where the Club does not hold the freehold). The Fixed Assets of a Club will include the Freehold if held, the remainder of the Lease if applicable, and such as: catering and office kit, books, pictures, silver, plate, furniture; the Current Assets will be stocks, debtors, bank balances and cash; the Current Liabilities will be creditors and taxation (as corporation tax levied on any bank interest or investment income). The Accounts might show some Investments (probably fixed-interest rather than equities) as a means of holding the various Reserves, especially any long-term Leasehold Sinking Fund.

The rating valuation of the Club will be on the basis that its purpose is not to make a profit (cf a proprietor's or commercially operated club) and the starting point will be the determination of the rental value of the premises – say, the Dorchester Hotel at £7m pa, the British Library at £12.7m, the Old Bailey at £3m, and Wormwood Scrubs at £1.5m (one guesses that Our Clubs will fall somewhere between the first and the last instances in terms of their facilities…). My Oxford college has a 2010 rateable value of a mere £150k, to which the 'poundage' of c50p is applied, and then with 80% relief for charities pays a negligible amount of c£15k pa – the highest valuation for a college is c£450k and the lowest c£75k, it being helpful to be old and derelict. The delayed 2015 revaluation, however, is likely to at least double valuations in the South of England and hence rates payable: this may have to be reflected by Clubs in member subscriptions.

Finally, a rather odd book by Andrew Graham (1957, Macmillan), 'The Club: A Novel', is a fictionalised guide to Club organisation, set in 'a big club in the heart of London's Clubland' ('the True Blue Club in St James's Street, London, England'). It makes many of the points already stressed in this Chapter about Club governance and management, and also as noted in Chapter 1 about the middle decades of the twentieth-century being economically very difficult for Clubland: 'a club is a business, needing and only sometimes getting, efficient direction and management'. The retiring Secretary is 'a damn bad Secretary' but at least 'he's a Sahib'; and the members of the General Committee (to whom 'inevitably the servants kow-towed') seek a replacement, trying to address 'the age-old question' – 'whether to entrust the management to an amateur or professional' (Oxbridge colleges used to go through the same process – a 'professional' Estates Bursar or one of the dons doing the job part-time…). The Club's (many difficult) members are described; the (dysfunctional) committee structure is explored ('anything of importance had to be submitted to this or that committee of well-meaning amateurs' leading to 'muddle and mediocrity') - the Library Committee being noted 'for the dreamlike and remoteness of its deliberations' over the Library as in fact 'the most charming [but] deserted backwater'; the AGM is explained. The new Secretary soon resigns in frustration; the Club eventually fails ('There was such a dead weight of monumental head in the sand and out-of-dateness.') and its (limited) assets are auctioned off. The Clubhouse becomes the corporate HQ of 'the Imperial Phosphates Company'… (Note also in similar vein Wintle, 1961, as cited in Chapter II.)

Chapter IV – The Club in Practice

Clubs – Mausoleums of inactive masculinity for men who prefer armchairs to women

V.S. Pritchett

The only place in London where my wife cannot get at me

Anon

Club – a weapon used by savages to keep white women at a distance

Anon

This Chapter explores the Clubs' customs and practices, layouts and facilities, activities and events; in short, what Griffiths (1907) calls 'Club Ways' in his Chapter IX – inter alia he discusses: 'the almost universal practice of snuff-taking, and its very slow replacement by the use of tobacco'; the admission of visitors-qua-'strangers'; the dress-code; and his Chapter XIV on 'The Inner Life of a Club' describes a twenty-four hour period and all the staff involved (a rhythm of daily Club-life still familiar, although now probably no Club still employs 'a professional quill-pen maker' – did one really do so in 1907?). His Chapter VIII is on 'Club Administration': a constant struggle to balance the books, the setting of subscriptions, staffing levels, stocking the wine-cellar, the kitchens, the importance of the Hall Porter ('often the most trusted and confidential of club servants' – Griffiths envisages this paragon perhaps judiciously protecting a member from debt-collectors by smuggling him out of the Clubhouse while they wait in the foyer). The Chapter goes on: the chef, the cashier... Chapter XIII ('The Ballot-Box') is specifically on the election process and the issue of black-balling. The thankless task of the Club Committee is noted (pp 195-201): 'an uncommonly hard part to play... suffers moral castigation perpetually... for ever assailed with grunts and grumbles and bitter reproaches... succeeds in pleasing nobody... an arduous, irksome, and too often ill-requited task...'.

The crucial role of a competent Club Secretary, working closely with an effective Club Management Committee, has already been explored in Chapter III, and today surely (hopefully) almost all of Our Clubs have cracked this problem of achieving efficient administration in terms of how in practice Our Clubs are run. There is now a network of Club Secretaries across Clubland busily sharing information, expertise, and experience - while being sensitive enough as the full-time official within each Club not to project too corporatist and bureaucratic an image. All in all, a not dissimilar role to that of the Home or Domestic Bursar in an Oxbridge college, or that of the Clerk of a Worshipful Livery Company, or even that of the Under-Treasurer of an Honourable Inn of Court – each having to patiently 'serve' a vociferous, articulate, intelligent membership made up of the sane and the less sane by way of the demands imposed, behaviour exhibited, foibles displayed, while also trying to staff a service-based organisation and keep it solvent as well as compliant with ever-expanding external regulation. Perhaps few Clubmen would disagree with the modern Club Secretary being described as a species in a similar way as this generous nineteenth-century comment on the Livery Company Clerk: 'We know scarcely any position which requires so much power of adaptability in its occupier as that of a clerk to a City company... much of [a company's] prestige and dignity depend upon his qualifications... [clerks] may be said to be of a far higher type than mere office drudges, and may rank among the higher class of educated and intelligent men.' (Palfreyman, 2010, p 259) – although there may well be the odd Oxbridge don unable to be quite so kind in assessing the worth of the modern full-time 'professional' Bursars of his/her College!

As also for the Livery Companies and the Oxbridge Colleges the standard of catering has improved dramatically in recent decades, and, although old-favourites by way of Nursery puddings (happily) still appear on Club menus, the style of cuisine has changed somewhat from the wide-range of recipes given in McDouall (1974) – note also the deliciously boozy 'Claret Jelly' from Edinburgh's New Club. And, thankfully, the turtle feasts (as also hugely popular in the nineteenth-century Livery Companies) have disappeared – see Timbs (1866, pp 70/1) re the Royal Society Club's turtle fetish in the 1780s.

On Club catering, the Kitchen hierarchy, from Head Chef to Demi Chef de Partie, is set out on p 16 of *Recipes from the Reform* (2014), along with the recipe for 'Lamb Cutlets Reform' (p 62) and 'Reform Trifle' (p 94) – for the latter we note it includes 'sherry to taste (optional)' but wander whether a temperance trifle has ever been served in the Reform... (having presented the New College Chef with a copy of this recipe book, I often order Reform Trifle for my private bursarial dinners at College, and always urge the Chef to be very heavy-handed with the sherry!). The Kitchens at the Reform are fundamentally unchanged since laid out by its 'Victorian celebrity chef' Alexis Soyer in the 1840s, he having become Head Chef at 27 and there having been thirteen Head Chefs since 1837 (p 128). Soyer (1809-1858), 'cook' and the 'Mirobolant' in

Thackeray's 'Pendennis', left Paris in 1830, became the Reform chef in 1837, organised the victualling of the military hospitals in the Crimean War, and wrote several cookery books (the *DNB*).

Carter's 2016 novel, 'The Devil's Feast, features the Reform Club and its famous Chef, as well as its Secretary and its Steward in the plot (see the entry for Carter in Chapter II on The Clubs in Literature). There is a lengthy description of a tour of the then new and then very high-tech Kitchens (pp 54-60): the visitors laugh, in disbelief and astonishment, when told that 'Monsieur Soyer believes that, one day, there will be a gas-stove in every kitchen in England'. As Carter notes, Soyer 'was the first celebrity chef'; Thackeray raved about his bacon and beans, but he also produced exotic dishes: desserts made to look like a lamb! In the novel he has 'a stormy relationship' with the Club Committee as Carter's plot unfolds – 'a mysterious and horrible death at the Reform, London's newest and grandest gentlemen's club… [in which there is] a web of rivalries and hatreds, both personal and political, simmering behind the Club's handsome façade'. Reading Carter's accounts of Reform Club feasts makes one long for simple cottage pie and peas, jam roly-poly and custard!

Neither the 1974 nor the 2014 above books on Club-grub feature 'the club popularity of marrow': 'Marrow-bones, clothed in snowy white napkins with the necessary silver accompaniments, already an institution of the place, were always ordered by the historian Gibbon when he dined at Boodle's.' (Escott, 1914, p 199). Escott also refers to 'the Garrick steak' as a Porterhouse-steak seemingly marinated in gin (p 257).

Wilson (2002, pp175/176), by the way, tells us that M. Alexis Soyer, 'as well as being a cook to the famous and to the greatest of the new Liberal clubs, was also a man who cared for the unfortunate'. He had developed soup kitchens in Ireland and had 'pioneered a practical stove' which he also took off to the Crimean War, using recipes from his 'Shilling Cookery' (1854). Inter alia: 'One of his best inventions was a gigantic vegetable cake' involving a hundredweight of mixed veg made into a dried cake that could reach the Crimea and then be divided into portions that were 'steamed into life when needed'! Out in the Crimea he met Mary Seacole, the self-trained nurse bringing better medical care to the troops - as also did, more famously, Florence Nightingale.

The configuration of Clubhouses and the naming of rooms or zones within them, as well as the sometimes arcane rules, are issues explored in the novel 'Clubbed to Death' (1992, Ruth Dudley Edwards): 'from all one hears about featherstonehaugh's, [it seems] to have been uncommonly keen on rules and regulations, even by the standard of gentlemen's clubs, all of which, as you probably know, are absolutely hide-bound by daft conventions, rules and nomenclatures. You know the sort of thing: it's true of most of them. The dining-room is called the Coffee Room, but it's the place where you can't have coffee. The place you sit in after lunch is likely to be called the Morning Room. The cold food restaurant is called the Strangers' Room because a hundred years ago you couldn't take strangers into the Coffee Room. The room with all the books in it isn't called the library, it's called the Smoking Room. And so on and so on...' (p 12). As Dudley Edwards comments: 'This is a way of confusing the new boys as well as the outsiders and making members feel superior and part of a private conspiracy.'.

And the complicated Clubhouse layout is also illustrated by the following extracts from the Members' Guide to one Club's facilities: 'The Coffee Room: 'Coffee Room' is the traditional designation for a London club's principal dining room... New members may find the ordering process in the Coffee Room a little unusual, but it is traditional and it works. After being shown to your table, the waiter will bring you the menu, the wine list and the bill on which to write your name and choice of dishes for yourself and any guests. The same slip should be used to order drinks. Puddings, cheese, savouries and digestifs are ordered orally later.'. The Rules continue: 'Top coats, umbrellas and gentlemen's hats are not permitted in the Club's public rooms and, unless taken to a bedroom, must be left in one of the three cloakrooms.'. The guidance continues: 'The Club exists for social reasons. However, its affairs are conducted with proper regard to members' changing requirements and so, in order to maintain the important tradition that business is not transacted in the major public rooms, the Pall Mall Room and the Lower Sitting Room have been extensively remodelled to form a comfortable, efficient and well-equipped Business Area... Documents may be taken into the Business Area and, if carried in one of the transparent plastic folders available from the Front Desk, the Libraries. They must not be taken into or displayed in other public rooms, such as the Morning Room, Coffee Room or Drawing Room.'. This Club's dress-code is perhaps 'more liberal' than that in many, and members are urged to 'interpret the code with a liberal quantity of common sense': in essence 'a jacket and tie' and 'commensurate formality' for women; 'less formality' at weekends (even jeans, but not 'shorts, t-shirts and trainers' which are simply 'never acceptable'); jackets can be removed 'in certain circumstances' (for instance, in the Business Area or while playing billiards, and 'on account of exceptionally hot weather' as formally declared when 'a notice to this effect has been placed in the Front Hall'), but only if in a long-sleeve shirt 'fastened at the cuff'. Exceptions apply when in 'the Squash Bar' or for 'anyone wearing National Dress'. And the Front Desk keeps a discrete 'supply of jackets and ties for loan to those who arrive under-equipped'.

The Clubs, with the exception of the extensive art collection held by the Garrick (see Ashton (1997) for a 600 page 'Catalogue of the

Paintings, Drawings, Watercolours and Sculpture' the Club owns), probably do not hold the historic artefacts that fill up some of the Halls of the Livery Companies or the Inns of Court (Palfreyman, 2010 & 2011), but they do own a range of interesting cartoons as explored in the book from the Cartoon Museum (2009) . Here we find 'hidden gems that hang on the walls of London's private clubs', among which are 'some of the best in private hands in Britain'. They include works by Bateman, Beerbohm, Cruikshank, Gillray, Heath Robinson, Hogarth, 'Jak', Low, Rowlandson, Steadman, and 'Vicky'. Some of Osbert Lancaster's Clublife cartoons are reproduced on pp 12/13 of Lejeune (2012) – usually featuring overweight elderly gents in dinner-jackets having some difficulty coming to terms with one aspect or other of the modern world...

As noted in the Introduction it is beyond the scope of this book even to list all the many Club histories with their endless anecdotes of the oddities of various Club members, and still less to provide a potted history of each Club – their websites do this job as do their Wiki entries. Suffice here to take a glance at just a couple of such histories – on 'The Athenaeum' (1975) and Thole (1992) on the Oxford and Cambridge Club; as well as at two editions of Lejeune on the whole range of Clubs, the latest (2012) and the third edition (1997). Burton's design and layout for the Athenaeum's 1830 Clubhouse (built for £35,000 and furnished for £4,000 – about £3m and around £300k in 2015 pounds) is typical of many later versions; while even the Club furniture can become iconic as in the sort of chairs associated with Our Clubs as 'club chairs' - Decimus Burton (1800-1881) also laid out Hyde Park. From Thole we learn that the O&C in 1975 was harbouring 25,000 bottles of Claret in its cellars and 13,000 bottles of Port – and that, back in the nineteenth-century, a Club butler had made off with 2,000 bottles over a number of years (by comparison, the New College SCR cellars currently shelter some 35,000 bottles of wine and about 2,500 bottles of port – a 'port lake' inherited from the quaffing habits of 1950s and 1960s male dondom now having been drained to manageable pond-like proportions and modern needs/tastes).

Other architects associated with Our Clubs include Sir Robert Smirke (1781-1867): his 1836 Clubhouse accommodates what is now the Oxford and Cambridge Club – another famous work is the Reading-Room of the British Museum; and Sir Reginald Theodore Blomfield (1856-1942), who restored Chequers and built Lambeth Bridge as well as contributing the new 1907 grand Suffolk Street premises of the Oxford and Cambridge University Club, now the HQ of Notre Dame University's Law School in London – an article by Blomfield on his Suffolk Street Clubhouse is reproduced in the Compendium of Images by kind permission of Professor Geoffrey Bennett, Director of London Law School (and a Member of the Oxford and Cambridge Club). In fact, Blomfield also reworked parts of the 1836 Smirke Clubhouse in the 1900s. Sir Charles Barry (1795-1860) was the architect for the 1831 Clubhouse of the Travellers Club - and the 1837 Reform Club as elsewhere noted (fortunately his Clubs' jobs did not overrun as badly as the Houses of Parliament – by 25 years and three times the original budge: Shenton, 2016). Wilson (2002, p 63) comments that Barry in his architecture was 'creating just that blend of serviceability and fantasy which are the hallmarks of imaginative buildings': 'The gentlemen who joined the Travellers enjoyed feeling that they were still on the Grand Tour, stepping from the dust of Pall Mall into the echoing hall and high-ceilinged domicile of some old Roman family of aristocratic lineage.'. Sir Alfred Waterhouse (1830-1905) was the architect for the National Liberal Club (1884) and the Natural History Museum ('which exhibits an unwonted exuberance of detail' – the *DNB*), as well as Manchester Town Hall (1877), the Pru's Holborn HQ, Balliol's Hall, the Oxford Union, and Salford Prison. The splendid architecture of Clubland spilled over into Brunel's 'grandly conceived' vision for the GWR refreshment rooms at Swindon: 'The finishes in the first-class [rooms] evoked the civilised luxury of the fashionable clubs of Pall Mall, with columns and pilasters in the imitation marble known as scagliola, a ceiling of ornate plasterwork, and walls painted in the manner of Italian Renaissance palaces.' (Bradley, 2015, pp 473/474) – a far cry indeed from the station buffet in 'Brief Encounter' let alone what we encounter today!

Did these grand edifices of Our Clubs ever see social unrest and risk invasion by the Great Unwashed? It seems that the closest they have (so far) come to riot if not revolution was on 8th February 1886 when up to 10,000 unemployed folk mingled with the socialists of William Morris's Socialist League were 'marching down Pall Mall towards Hyde Park, past the grandiose club buildings of London' (Wilson, 2002, pp 445/6): 'As they passed the Liberal Reform Club, the servants pelted the unemployed with shoes [whose?!] and nail-brushes. The marchers returned the hoots and jeers of the clubmen and their servants, and by the time they had turned the corner into St James's Street, tempers were high. The Tories of the Carlton Club jeered at them and soon found metal bars and paving stones hurtling through the broken glass of the club windows.' On 13th November the next year there was a similar massive demonstration in nearby Trafalgar Square, where the crowds faced 2,000 police backed up cavalry and giving rise to at least 3 deaths and some 200 being injured among the protestors (Vallance, 2009, p 461).

Lejeune (1997) starts with 'the good news from clubland': 'no more major losses' by way of Clubs closing (compared with the losses recorded in the 1979 and 1984 editions); 49 Clubs (not all in Pall Mall and St James's) are then portrayed. For the 2012 edition the fly-leaf reads: 'Clubland is another country... either luxurious or a bit shabby... offering wine and food at various levels of delight and disappointment... '; and with 'over 360 exclusive photographs and archival pictures' it is indeed 'a book to treasure'. This time 31 Clubs are featured – including 3 City Clubs – and it is declared that 'London's clubland flourishes' and 'Clubland continues to blossom': 'A new will to live the good life in the honoured English way has emerged.'. The Club remains a 'peculiarly English institution' with London as 'the mother city of clubs'. The entry for White's declares it to have 'a good claim to be considered the archetype and model of what a gentlemen's club should be' (p 225). Lejeune on p 234 sets out a poem on 'Clubs' as 'Turned by a female hand' that neatly illustrates the concerns explored in Chapter I about the Club's impact on the domestic bliss of married life: it contains lines like, 'We hate the name of Clubs!', 'The Wretches... live, eat, drink, at Clubs!', 'They're married to their Clubs.'.

A final look at Lejeune (2012, p 237): he has a splendid extract from Nevill's 'London Clubs' (1911) which is headed 'The Perfect Clubman': 'there is [in most Clubs] to be found some member who is generally recognised as an institution of the place... likes to read the same newspaper in the same place... lunch at the same time.. have his dinner served at the same hour in the same corner of the coffee-room... [he] knows everything that is going on... his conversation is generally amusing and occasionally instructive... The life of such a man, as has been said, is centred in his club... it would require an invasion or an earthquake to make him change his habits. So he lunches and dines, dines and lunches, till the sands of the hourglass have run out, and the moment comes for him to enter that great club of which all humanity must perforce become members.'.

I had intended to resist filling this little book on Our Clubs with the (rather tedious) anecdotes about Clublife and eccentric Clubmen that tend to swamp the books on Clubland from earlier eras (see those listed in the Preface; and, of course, the many histories of individual Clubs listed in the Bibliography are replete with such anecdotes), but perhaps the job would not be properly done without here recording a few of the tales that surround any discussion of Clubland, these being the ones that, it seems to me, are consistently and widely recycled over the decades:

- In Boodle's some Members (supposedly) took time to adjust to the installation of modern sanitation and hence, ever-attentive to the whims of the membership, for a while chamber-pots remained readily available.
- It was (seemingly) also Boodle's that boiled coins before giving them as change to Members – not served hot as revenge by staff upon rude members but for reasons of sanitary advantage (somewhat at odds with anecdote one above).
- All Clubs (apparently) used to iron the newspapers.
- F.E. Smith, Earl of Birkenhead, is said, on his walk over to the Lords, to have regularly popped into the Athenaeum to make use of its sanitary facilities. Challenged one day by the doorman asking him whether he was a Member, he responded: 'Good Grief! Is this a Club as well?'. An alternative version, doubtless put around by Athenaeum Members, is that it was the National Liberal Club which Smith mistook for a rather grand public convenience.
- Over at the Beefsteak Club the comings and goings of gents attracted Police interest and a raid on what was assumed to be dodgy premises led to Police asking one by one a table of Members who they were: back the answers duly came, one by one, as the Lord Chancellor, the Governor of the Bank of England, and so on. The Police, disbelieving, asked the next

The Club in Practice

in turn: 'And I assume you are the Prime Minister?'. 'Well, yes.', responded Arthur Balfour. Perhaps this anecdote is conclusive evidence of Our Clubs at least at some time being the centre of Establishment power-broking as discussed in Chapter I and in the Conclusion?

- A Minister in Attlee's second (1951) Labour (indeed Socialist) Government, Aneurin Bevan, unwisely ventured into Clubland, having declared that all Tories were 'lower than vermin'. On being taken into White's by a Member, another Member attempted to kick Bevan down the Clubhouse steps, missed, and resigned (whether for failure to make impact or for a breach of Club etiquette is unclear, although failure was excusable since the individual had lost a leg in the War). All this duly gave rise to various Osbert Lancaster cartoons in the *Daily Express*.

- The practice of the Members from a Club closed for its August break being taken in at other Clubs gives us the story that two chaps from the Guards' Club were taking refuge in the Oxford and Cambridge. Looking around at their plush surroundings, one commented loudly to the other that: 'These middle-class fellows do themselves well.'. A newspaper (hopefully adequately ironed) was lowered by a nearby gent ensconced in a leather club-chair, revealing the Duke of Wellington, war-hero and Chancellor of Oxford University.

- In the 1960s 'Hetty's Bar' in the Oxford and Cambridge Club was home to a parrot called Lorita, belonging to an elderly judge who resided at the Clubhouse.

- A notice at a Club read: 'Members are requested not to bring their mistresses into the Club unless they happen to be the wives of other members.'

- And from Algy Cluff (*Unsung Heroes* 2018) a tale of H. 'Loopy' Whitbread as 'one of the more extraordinary ornaments of clubland in the 1950s and 1960s', he being 'of fairly repulsive appearance, with pendulous jowls and a large paunch' and who 'appeared to have had two eggs for breakfast – one of which he had eaten and the other he had smeared over his Old Etonian tie'. He lived alone and bussed into his club every day, enquiring on arrival whether there were any letters for him – invariably there was at least one, and often only the one, which he had posted the day before! His 'only subject was Eton College, about which he knew everything…'.
- The Reader should feel free to add his or her own favourite anecdote…
- Or two.

Finally, referring back to our History of the Clubs in Chapter I and our noting there that the coffee-houses and the societies emerging in London in the Restoration decades were similarly seen in both Oxford generally and also in its colleges in the form of the early SCRs, now a little more on the Oxford SCR and the JCR in practice (and ignoring Cambridge as a less significant and sociable place, although the Combination Room as the equivalent of the Oxford SCR may well have emerged even earlier than in 1661 at Merton, 1665 at Trinity, and 1678 at New College). Volume VII(2) of the 10,000 page monumental 'The History of the University of Oxford' (the nineteenth-century being covered by Brock & Curthoys, 2000) comments on the development of student clubs and societies from mid-century, centred on sport and debating, that then became 'the model for and even the origin of' the JCRs (pp 149/151): 'There is no more distinctive feature of modern college life than the JCR.', declared the undergraduate magazine (the *JCR*) in 1897, just as the late-Victorian and the Edwardian expansion of Our Clubs was in full swing). In fact, while most colleges saw their JCRs begin in the 1860s or so, the New College JCR had started in the 1680s and Pembroke's celebrated its first hundred years in 1894.

Similarly, Brockliss (2016) in his magnificent one-volume 850-page history of the University of Oxford comments on 'the creation of the seniors' own social space' in the 1660s-1680s (p 288) and of the JCRs in the 1870s/1880s (pp 457/8) – the latter often having a JCR Steward as 'a long-serving figure of mythical proportions' and 'known to generations of undergraduates for his knowledge of college lore and sound advice' (the London Club's Hall Porter in the later decades of the nineteenth-century and on into the twentieth-century seems to have fulfilled a similar role and had much the same status). Brockliss comments that, while not all dons in the eighteenth-century and through into the early decades of the next century were 'indolent alcoholics', some certainly enjoyed to the full the SCR facilities: 'At Queen's in 1811 they got through 1,470 bottles of port... At Magdalen in 1741-2, one William Henchman received £38 2s 7d for his fellowship but owed the college [more than twice that amount at] £91 13s 6d [for his SCR booze].' (pp 290-292) – by the way, dondom still pays personally for its SCR and High Table imbibing (although few now would incur Henchman's modern equivalent of an £18k bill against their salary - even at the current rate of c£65-85k depending on the wealth of the College).

The fledgling Oxford JCRs of the second-half of the nineteenth-century, however, initially faced an uncertain future: 'Constituted as private clubs, they were regarded by the authorities as a source of extravagance and idleness.' (Brock & Curthoys, 2000). Although New College's JCR was long-established by the late-1860s the dons felt 'the expensive annual subscription (6 guineas)' was a threat to their expansion plans since it was too costly for poor students (a concern even back then about what we now call 'access' and 'widening participation' in the politics of higher education – Palfreyman & Tapper, 2014; Palfreyman & Temple, 2017). The New College Governing Body also expressed anxiety about 'the inappropriate style of social life which the JCR encouraged, illustrated by damning statistics of champagne consumption' (the New College JCR was clearly more modelled on the Savage Club than the Reform or the Athenaeum), at a time when the colleges were beginning to take their teaching duties seriously and to establish what we today see as 'The Oxford Tutorial' teaching methodology (Palfreyman, 2008). The GB sought an Opinion from Lord Chief Justice Erle (naturally a New College Old Member) – this hand-written document, still safely in the College's Muniment Tower, duly opined that the GB owned the property of the JCR (a lot of port, and 'a few books'), that the JCR 'had no right or any colourable claim over these items', and hence the GB could indeed close it down (para 9.04 of Farrington & Palfreyman, 2012). The JCR threatened to move offshore into rented space in Holywell Street, but a compromise was eventually brokered by Bursar Alfred Robinson. Much the same dispute happened over at Magdalen, and by the 1890s all colleges except unclubbable Corpus possessed a JCR.

Brock & Curthoys (p 751) note that generally the SCRs were rather Spartan: 'sanded floors and spittoons had not given way to carpets until early in the [twentieth-]century', and the Senior Fellow of Exeter College in 1894 announced that he would not set foot in the place if the SCR gained a carpet; it did and he did not ('Gentlemen, if you will introduce such a monstrous luxury, I will never enter this room again.'). In the case of New College (certainly not now noted, thankfully, for having a Spartan SCR) a chandelier ordered, presumably in a fit of donnish exuberance, in the 1850s for its Panelled Room 'was found still packed in its maker's box' in the

1930s; it now hangs there proudly (if rather dimly). Thus, there seems to have been a touch of Cambridge puritanism even among Oxford's royalist dondom, and certainly compared to the search for tasteful opulence in Our Clubs during the 1890s/1900s. That said, the New College Victorian Fellows did solve a major health & safety problem in how to keep the claret and port circulating, given that there was a risk of don and (more worryingly) bottle falling into the roaring log fire as the former tottered across the gap in the horseshoe of small tables and their clusters of chairs focussed on the fireplace: the ingenious answer, using gravity and pulleys, was dreamt up by Warden Shuttleworth in the 1830s and is the 'Shuttleworth Port Railway' still in constant activity, he explaining that he had seen the principle of the inclined plane in use in the collieries of his native Durham. Thus, the New College SCR Members had identified and duly assessed a H&S risk and had addressed it with an effective 'risk management plan', and so they could safely continue with 'the tradition of a dignified and mellow conviviality' begun in 1678 (and as mimicked, sans a port railway, in a block of rooms built opposite a decade later for the JCR) – A.H. Smith, 1952, 'New College and its Buildings', pp 92-94).

Conclusion – The Clubs in Future?

The Club as *a refuge from the vulgarity of the outside world, a reassuringly fixed point, the echo of a civilised English way of life*

Anthony Lejeune, 'The Gentlemen's Clubs of London', 2012

In Chapter I we left the History of the Clubs at around 1990 and now, in considering the current and future role of Clubland in this new century, let us begin by seeing what Anthony Sampson (1992, 2004) has to say about whether they continue to host the Establishment as, according to Paxman (1990) and Scott (1991), they once did – although, as we saw in Chapter I, Sampson himself envisaged a crumbling in this aspect of their significance even in his 1965 second edition. By the time of his 1992 update to the iconic 'Anatomy of Britain' the Index contains no mention of 'Clubs and Clubland' let alone a whole chapter as in the 1965 edition. The same applies to the 2004 latest edition. Seemingly the Establishment (a concept 'which caused such excitement and indignation forty years ago', p 348) has moved on, just as 'The ideal of the English gentleman [has] evaporated' (p 343) – see also Annan (1990) on his generation's reacting against 'the insufferable ideal' by way of 'the gospel of the gentlemen' as 'the official code of the public schools' (chapters 2 and 3). Moreover, even if the top civil servants are still able to afford the cost of and the time for lunching and dining in their Clubs (see Chapter I and also Chapter II re the 'Yes Minster' era), these chaps (and indeed now chapesses) no longer matter anyway (they are 'suffering from their own loss of confidence and status, in decline since their heyday after the second world war' – Sampson, 2004, p 110).

Nor are the Permanent Secretaries alone in perhaps still lunching in the Athenaeum but not being of significance in Sampson's terms of 'Who Runs this Place?': the same applies to Vice-Chancellors since academia has become 'dependent and demoralised' (p 206), while the Bishops are today an irrelevance compared to their glory days of aprons and top-hats in Trollope's Athenaeum. Indeed, the Index reference to 'Clubs and Clubland' had disappeared as early as the 1971 third edition of the 'Anatomy', as also for the 1982 update. And by 2004 'the circles of Britain's power-centres look very different from the pattern of forty years ago', with 'the new Establishment' being based simply on 'the colour of money' (pp 354/5) and not to be found plotting and scheming over the port in our Clubland (although it might be hitting the cocktails over at a fashionable new proprietor club such as Soho House?) . Certainly, Our Clubs are not, and never have been, part of a secretive Establishment in the way that the Freemasons have been seen over the centuries; and nor are they a closed world in the way that in the USA university campus fraternity 'Greek life' really does seems to permeate later civic and political life – assuming the student members survive the bizarre (and sometimes deadly) 'hazing' rituals during 'pledging' that make the antics even of Oxford's Bullingdon Club look like a Sunday School outing (DeSantis, 2007).

Tombs (2014), however, comments in relation to 'The Establishment': its institutions and manifestations, 'after faltering, proved remarkably resilient and adaptive. It would have been hard to imagine during the 1960s that, half a century on, the monarchy would be revered, the public schools booming, gentlemen's clubs expanding, the armed forces above criticism, the Prime Minister an Etonian [Cameron], and Cambridge and Oxford hailed as Europe's leading universities. Like much in England, they changed and remained the same.' (p 791). Indeed, as Annan (1990, p 14) noted: 'But the Establishment is protean; it can change its shape.'. King (2015) sees a 1950s 'centralized and power-hoarding system' as also 'a highly establishmentarian system' where 'the business of governing' was 'to be left in the hands of persons equipped by background, training and temperament to perform that task' (pp 16/17) – a collective of thoroughly sound-chaps, each blessed with a safe-pair-of-hands and all sharing common values imbued at public schools, in Oxbridge colleges, and within Our Clubs. Over subsequent decades, however, 'a far larger number of organised interests' emerges and (King here quoting Grant, 2000) we end up with 'pressure-group politics' replacing 'the Establishment dominated era of the 1950s', and hence with a far more open, messy, and fuzzy political process (p 131). Like Sampson, he views 'the British civil-service machine' as a casualty of this change – perhaps still a Rolls-Royce whose 'minders take care to polish it lovingly' but one now where 'the rust is beginning to corrode the wheel arches, and the clutch is slipping [while] the brakes may be dangerously faulty' (p 197): 'The system is certainly less establishmentarian than it was.' (p 278). And in answer to the title of his book, 'Who Governs Britain?', King's reply is 'no one institution and certainly no one individual' (p 287) – perhaps a new version of an Establishment, but now located elsewhere than in Pall Mall, and probably in cyber-space? As Jones (2015, p 12) comments: 'The Establishment is a shape-shifter, evolving and adapting as needs must.'. For an entertaining skewering of what a *Daily Mail* journalist sees as the modern Establishment there is Letts (2017) who identifies a network of the 'snooterati', of 'Guardianistas', of quango-fodder PC-preachers, of 'patronising Remoaners' focussed upon 'London's club-class elite'. He adds that 'One of the pleasures of writing for the *Mail* is that it makes Establishment bores so terribly cross' (p 297).

Yet so what if the new century finds the Establishment (if it really ever existed and if it still exists) clubbing (if anywhere at all) elsewhere than in our Clubland (see Jones, 2015, who certainly does not find it ensconced in Pall Mall or St James's) - so long as 'Our Clubs' can survive financially as social and recreational venues without seeking (if indeed they ever consciously did) to be extensions of 'the corridors of power' (wherever they may now be – Canary Wharf boardrooms?): but see Kendall (2008) on elite clubs in the USA as haunts of the American version of the Establishment. Can we discover more about the 2015 pulse of Our Clubs from a Google search under, say, Club, Clubs, Clubland? Well, we get the websites for many of Our Clubs (and for other less desirable entities) as well as being directed to a lot of 'clubland' popular culture and entertainment. Searching for 'gentlemen's clubs' is asking for trouble, flagging up a great deal of interesting but for our purposes irrelevant entries/sites…

And, more helpfully, the search generates also some newspaper articles that perpetuate the Clubland image of 'gruff old coves snoozing in wing chairs after lunches of dreadful food and excellent claret' (the *Express* under 'The secret world of gentlemen's clubs' on 24/1/14) . Other material explores the old topic of admitting women as members of certain of Our Clubs, such as the *Guardian* (30/4/15) under 'Time, gentlemen: when will the last all-male clubs admit women?' – 'The Garrick Club in London is preparing for a bitter struggle over whether to admit women members. How long can the British establishment fend off modernity?'. In this *Guardian* article Max Hastings, 'a passionate defender of gentlemen's clubs', is quoted as seeing them as 'extremely pleasant backwaters [having] nothing at all to do with real life in Britain in the C21st century' (so, not harbouring the Establishment then). He declares that he likes 'the mustiness of clubs', full of 'peculiar, quirky old men'. The *Telegraph* (11/7/15, 'Gentlemen's clubs should stay as they are') unsurprisingly sides with Hastings rather than the *Guardian* (or indeed with Prime Minister Cameron who had resigned from White's in 2013 over this issue).

In *The Times* (15/10/11) the 'contempt' of Baroness Hale, the only female member of the UK Supreme Court, for the Garrick's male-only rule is featured ('Men-only mentality puts the Garrick in contempt of a Supreme Court judge'), the then row triggered by Joanna Lumley being proposed for membership by Hugh Bonneville. (The *Times*, 15/9/17, p 40, noted that the Anglo-German Club, Hamburg, retains its male-only membership restriction as a Club founded by British Army officers in 1948 and now said to be 'attracting the cream of Hamburg [male] society and their lady guests' to its 'grand villa' that 'looks like a carbon copy of a gentleman's club in Pall Mall' – two dozen 'young' members had publicly called for review of the male-only policy but the Club President is reported as saying that 'no women have ever made requests to become members'. Baroness Hale also commented (*Sunday Times* 26/11/17, p 29) that judges should not be members of clubs such as the Garrick since it means they have 'automatically got access to gossip that people who can't be there don't have' (the *ST* wonders if, were the Garrick to admit female members, 'won't the men just gossip in the gents instead' – well, perhaps the Garrick could go for unisex loos?!).

The same Google search finds us a link to a 'YouTube' 2010 clip from the US cartoon series, 'Family Guy', where three gents in front of a roaring Clubland fireside 'communicate' by coughing and sputtering from behind their (broadsheet – the *Telegraph* perhaps) newspapers, reaching a crescendo and then subsiding – thereby demonstrating the abiding media stock-image of Our Clubs. I am unable to ascertain whether that other famous American cartoon series, 'The Simpsons', has ever featured the London gentlemen's clubs – if not, clearly, Homer and family should be given a pretext to visit Pall Mall… Finally, there is a 'Political history of gentlemen's clubs' as a BBC 'Daily Politics' film (22/1/16): it awards Our Clubs, still, a role in the 'political discourse' of modern times as 'a plotter's paradise'.

This is a theme echoed in a *Financial Times* article (21/12/12, 'Gentlemen's clubs savour sweet success') , which declares that 'the grandest clubs retain their attraction as unofficial meeting places for influential people'. They are deemed to have moved well beyond 'the stereotype [as] a place of fusty exclusivity, where elderly gents snooze in leather armchairs beside marble fireplaces'; they are 'thriving', with club cuisine 'once derided for its resemblance to school dinners' duly 'transformed'. The article lists 'Who's where?' – inter alia, Mervyn King is a member of the Athenaeum, Brooks's, and the Garrick; George Soros of Brooks's; Boris Johnson of the Beefsteak; and Lord Patten of the Athenaeum, the RAC, and the Oxford & Cambridge. And the *FT* returns to its fixation with Our Clubs as venues for political intrigue: 'Of all London's streets, Pall Mall is the most Roman in style – a grand, broad canyon lined by palazzo style 19th century members' clubs. Each building offers a marmoreal refuge for the covert business of politicians and other wielders of influence – one in which portraits of their predecessors line the walls.' (26/1/16, 'The noble art of a mason').

But, if the Establishment is still comfortably ensconced within Our Clubs, as opposed to having relocated elsewhere or even already disintegrated (as speculated earlier in this volume), what of its future? If by the Establishment we mean a cosy governing globalised exam-passing elite used to getting its way over a broadly liberal social and political agenda while carefully ignoring life north of Watford (except perhaps for Oxford and Cambridge), then Eatwell & Goodwin (2018) makes scary reading for these folk in the London bubble – they chart the rise of 'national populism' as 'the revolt against liberal democracy' in the USA (Trumpism), the UK (Brexit), France, Italy, Poland, Hungary, Germany, even The Netherlands and Sweden. They predict it is here to stay and note that it should not be surprising given, say, the attitude of the EU Brussels bureaucratic elite shown by the quotes they give from over the decades of the march of the EU Project: for example, Jean Rey, former President of the European Commission: 'A referendum on this matter [the UK joining in 1974] consists of consulting people who don't know the problems instead of consulting people who know them. I would deplore a situation in which the policy of this great country should be left to housewives.' (pp 98/99; while the Chief of Staff to the current President is quoted as dismissing the 2016 Brexit vote as 'stupid'). That same President, Mr Juncker, is quoted as smugly declaring in the late-1990s: 'We decree something, then float it and wait some time to see what happens. If no clamour occurs and no big fuss follows, because most people do not grasp what has been decided, we continue – step by step, until the point of no return is reached.' (p 100).

Otherwise, Our Clubs really receive very little attention from the media – and none of it is aggressive or damaging. Indeed, the Clubs are often portrayed as a tad dull: Harry Mount, in profiling 'former *Spectator* owner' and 'unlikely oilman' Algy Cluff, declares that, although Cluff's 'Who's Who' entry 'lists membership of 11 clubs', 'there is no clubman stuffiness about him' (*Spectator*, 30/4/16). Searching under Google's 'News' filter features nothing more than 'a drunken fracas' at the Reform Club when Nigel Farrage arrived (the *Daily Mail* on 6/4/14) and, supposedly, upset some of its more liberal members; there is also 'Treasurer of historic private members' club stole more than £500,000' concerning the East India Club (the *Telegraph* on 26/8/14) . The Reform again gets press attention as 'one of London's grandest and most expensive clubs'

(£1580 pa membership) because of 'an unprecedented row after members rebelled against its ruling body over the appointment of a new club secretary' and asserting that at 66 the appointee to the £80k job was 'too old' and his naval background inappropriate by way of relevant experience, all as a 'revolt' in a Club 'marred by factionalism': *Times* (2/11/16); and also the *Daily Telegraph* (2/11/16) as 'Reform Club feud sinks retired commander', citing an 'extremely ill-tempered and petulant... absolutely shambolic' meeting and 'calls for the Committee to resign'.

The Hurlingham (albeit not strictly one of Our Clubs) made it to *The Times* (p 11, 28/7/18) concerning alleged 'bullying and email hacking' supposedly resulting from Members squabbling over the extent and cost of refurbishment plans – the plans then being rejected at the AGM and the Chair subsequently resigning, complaining of 'unacceptably rude' behaviour by some Members (*The* Times , p 13, 5/1/19) . And the Reform was (yet again) in the news more recently (*Sunday Times*, p 9, 6/5/18) re 'a flurry of lawsuits, allegations of blackmail and a trail of embarrassing revelations that led to the doorstep of one of London's grandest social institutions: the Reform Club in Pall Mall...' where seemingly the Club's Chairman had 'stood down unexpectedly [after] changes he introduced angered powerful members who [allegedly] leaked stories about him to the media...'. These lurid tales involved sadomasochism in 'dungeons' within houses in Chorley and Blackburn - locations somewhat remote, physically and socially, from St James's! While back in St James's the FT (26/1/19) reported on 'Niece's Night' at Buck's as, seemingly, an annual event where 'the mainly elderly membership [invite] women in their twenties [who are duly] rotated [with the courses] between tables'; quoted comments from the invitees on the evening range from 'very light-hearted' to 'vile'.

Still in Pall Mall, this time at the National Liberal Club, the 'crusties' have got upset at the idea that gents can remove their ties: 'one dinosaur roars' about being tieless signifying 'laziness or incompetence'; and another worried that 'string vests and flip-flops' will next be allowed: the *Times* (1/12/16, p 13), noting that Paddy Ashdown is tieless in his Club portrait. Another newspaper piece is by David Tang (*Financial Times*, 4/12/17) asking whether any reader would put Trump up for membership 'at one of your clubs', given that he 'wears his coat buttons unfastened [and also] his shiny monochrome ties several inches below his waistline'. Tang answers his own question - he would on the basis that his clubs seek to have 'a collection of members who are different and not one-dimensional' and that 'Trump will be a darn sight more interesting than the average member and should bring plenty of jollities, and I hope absurdities, to the club'. He continues: 'The days of clubs consisting of a large cosy network of old buffers are really nowadays confined to the cobweb corners of historic metropolises'. Can he possibly mean Our Clubland? And hence by the second-half of this new century will we find that the dominant model is once again the proprietor club? – the Athenaeum becomes a branch of Soho House, members asked to remove ties and jackets, jeans and trainers welcome. The National Liberal taken over by the National Trust, its coffee-room offering 'authentic' Club Grub (roast beef, tapioca pudding, Club Claret), an army of retired actors employed to shuffle around the premises as Old Buffers when not doing a stint dozing in the Library?

The entrepreneur and journalist, Luke Johnson, in his *Sunday Times* column (19/3/17, Business section, p 12) tells us he has 'always loved clubs' – 'Joining a club is a British habit, and London is the mother of clubs.' Folk join, he says, 'to network', 'for status', 'out of snobbery', 'to feel that we belong' – although our 'class system' is another reason 'we have embraced them so heartily in this country'.

The Clubs in Future?

He is a member of the Groucho as 'an alternative to the stuffy gentlemen's clubs of St James's'; and notes the more recent rise of Soho House and other 'business model' clubs (as opposed to 'the old-school clubs' as 'mutuals owned by their members') – pondering whether, in fact, London now faces 'peak club' with, 'at least 75 of these gathering places in central London'. Sadly, he feels he gets 'poor value' from his several clubs, which do not include the Garrick – he admits to having been blackballed by 'an old business colleague' (and, as it happens, he is tieless and prefers clubs 'that admit women'). But, he concludes: 'the urge to be a member of a club is a powerful one – and I shall not be resigning from my clubs just yet.'

Finally, in terms of exploring the image of Our Clubs in the media and in cyberspace and by way of exhaustive 'clicking' as the modern form of academic research there is Google 'Images' for 'gentlemen's clubs' where we get a splendid collection of photographs of the exteriors and the interiors of Our Clubs – albeit interspersed with images of semi-naked ladies who seemingly are the under-liveried staff of another kind of gentlemen's club to be found in some US states...

Thus, the media portrayal and the cyber-image of London's Pall Mall Clubs is really rather benign, as also for the London Livery Companies (Palfreyman, 2010) and only a tad less so for London's Inns of Court (Palfreyman, 2011): Oxford University and its colleges are not usually treated as gently by the media! On the Livery Companies there are similarly tolerant and almost affectionate comments: they 'still practice weird rituals straight out of *Gormanghast*' and their members 'dress up in medieval costume at every opportunity' while engaging in 'sometimes Ruritanian excesses'. The Inns' cyber-space image is a shade more edgy: there is an hilarious allegation that the Inns are part of a vast evil conspiracy linking them and the Masons plus MI5, while another crack-pot conspiracy is that the Inns are seeking global domination via the International Bar Association as a puppet organisation - well, I hope it is all conspiracy theory…

So, to conclude:

The Clubs thrive, Clubland is secure, Clubbery and the Clubocracy flourish. Our Clubs, their declining numbers having stabilised by the mid-1980s, are not, thankfully, suffering from the depressing 'Bowling Alone' trend towards 'atomised individualism' within US and UK society (Putnam, 2000, p 140 – in contrast to the earlier era described in Kaufman, 2002: and, cf, an estimate for Germany has half the population belonging to a social club, to some 600,000 'Vereine'). Other clubs and societies across the UK, however, may, sadly, be in relative decline as folk work longer hours, commute greater distances, and are distracted from regular social and associational gatherings by the lures of TV and other media forms – there seems to be no modern equivalent in our secular society of, say, the quaint 'spiritualised club movement' promoted in Butterworth's 1932 'Clubland' via the network of boys clubs across south London (and see also the young Clement Attlee's involvement with the Hailbury Club in Stepney during the 1900s as an example of such clubs: Bew, 2016, pp 50-53). Our Clubs remain 'Secret Places, Hidden Sanctuaries' (Klimczuk & Warner, 2009), but not any longer (if indeed ever) as haunts of Establishment plotters: more 'for the purpose of good fellowship and unabashed enjoyment', for escape from 'the pressures of the outside world' (their Introduction). In their chapter 13 ('Jolly Good Fellowship') they outline 'the history, characters, and rich anecdotage of those ultimate impenetrable sanctuaries: private clubs' – starting with 'the imposing array of aristocratic and highly eccentric clubs established in London' and 'the fund of lore, elegance, and humour residing in the still-flourishing clubs of London' (p 5). These authors stress what is stressed in this little book: the gentlemen's club 'is essentially an English invention', with a dominant media and public image based on 'an Edwardian vignette of discreet luxury' still surviving to some extent in today's Clubs, an image that 'amounts to an entire culture and mythology' and one that is extensively portrayed in literature. Long may Our Clubs survive and also thrive.

Appendices: List of Clubs Past, Present, New, and Fictional

Man is a social animal

Aristotle ('Politics')

A. Some Clubs Past

Albermarle Club, 1874-1941.

Almack's Club, Pall Mall, 1765 to 1867 (but refounded, 1908-1961) – in the early decades no member could also belong to Arthur's Club at Arthur's Chocolate House; the Macaroni Club met at the same premises until 1772. In its early decades it was a mixed club. Not to be confused with…

Almack's Assembley Rooms, King Street, which ran from 1765 into the later part of the C19.

American Club, 1919-1980s.

Arthur's Club, St James's Street, emerged from Arthur's Chocolate House in 1827 as a Club mainly for country gentlemen; survived until 1940.

Bachelors' Club, c1881-1946.

Bath Club, Brook Street, 1894-1981. Originally in Dover Street, complete with swimming-pool, until the Club-house was burned

Appendix

down in 1941 (despite the quantum of water it contained). Merged with the Conservative Club in 1950.

Civil Service Club – of which Trollope was a member (see Chapter II): but re-incarnated 1953: see below.

Cocoa Tree Club, Pall Mall, 1746 – evolving from the Cocoa Tree Chocolate House, 1698.

Crockford's Club, 1828-1845 (not to be confused with the extant Crockfords Casino in Curzon Street which claims to have inherited William Crockford's vision of what a gentlemen's club should be…).

Devonshire Club, 1875 – amalgamated in 1976 with the East India Club as below.

Marlborough Club, Pall Mall, 1869-1953: a tofts' club for the mates of Bertie, the Prince of Wales; initially including a bowling-alley. Allegedly, it was founded because Bertie had fallen out with the Committee of White's over the right to smoke in the Club's Morning Room. Smoking was allowed throughout the Marlborough Club.

Public Schools Club, 1909 until merged in 1972 with the East India Club as below.

St James's Club, Piccadilly, 1859-1975: absorbed the Dilettanti Society in 1922 and the Bachelors' Club in 1946, before itself merging with Brooks's as below.

Union Club, Carlton House Terrace (and many places before), 1799-1964.

United Service Club, Pall Mall, 1815-1976: amalgamated with the Junior United Service Club in 1953, and absorbed 400 members from the Union Club (as above) in 1964, as well as those of the Royal Aero Club in 1971.

Windham House Club, Pall Mall, 1828 – later the Windham Club in St James's Square until 1942 when effectively merged into the Travellers Club as below, but formally amalgamated in 1945 with the Marlborough Club as above.

Not in Clubland but listed anyway! The Club – later the Literary Club: haunt of Johnson, Reynolds, Goldsmith, Burke, Garrick (but Gibbon was initially rejected). Johnson also founded the Ivy lane Club in 1749. The Eccentric Club, 1890-1980s, for theatre types. The King of Clubs, 1801-1824, for monthly conversation. The Kit-Kat Club, 1700-1720, was a Whig political club. The Press Club, 1882-1986, moved around until crushing debt killed it off. The Prince's Sporting Club, latterly in Knightsbridge, also ran into hard times and folded during the War. The Whittington Club, Arundel Street, 1846, was a literary club. The Wig and Pen, Strand, closed in 2003.

A.I. Dasent (1920, Macmillan) in his *Piccadilly In Three Centuries* gives us in Chapter III on 'The Club-Houses of Piccadilly' (then threatening 'to become a serried mass of Club-houses') a list of such premises over the decades: the Royal Thames Yacht Club, the Naval and Military Club as 'the best managed club in London', the Junior Naval and Military Club (formerly the Junior Travellers), the St James's Club, the Junior Constitutional, the Isthmian Club, the British and Foreign Union Club ('a short-lived society' but perhaps, in the early-1830s, 'the first genuine club in Piccadilly'), the Savile Club, the Junior Athenaeum, the Automobile Club ('grown to be of gigantic proportions'), the Cavalry Club, the Bachelors' Club (aka 'Gillett's Blades'). Timbs (1866) has (rather tedious!) anecdotes of 'One Hundred Clubs'; while Graves (1963) gives sketches of some sixty clubs.

Appendix

More exotically, there was the Cannibal Club located safely away from Pall Mall and associated with the Anthropological Society in the 1860s; meeting in a Fleet Street banquet/dining-room (Bertolini's) this collective of what we would now label as sexist racists thought they 'knew' that 'primitives' were 'inferior' to European gents such as themselves and also believed in phrenology as well as a nice bit of flogging/flagellation (Lutz, 2011).

B. Clubs Present

Army and Navy Club, Pall Mall, 1837 – but various premises before settling into its newly-built Pall Mall home (modelled on a Venetian palace) by 1848; as rebuilt in 1963. Often known as 'the Rag' – see the entry under Thackeray in Chapter II.

Arts Club, Dover Street, 1863, and merged with the Authors' Club in 1976. Famous members include Dickens, Kipling, Mark Twain, Trollope, Irving.

Athenaeum, Pall Mall, 1824 – said to be the most intellectually elite of all London's clubs, initially known as 'The Society'. Where in 'Yes Minister' and 'Yes Prime Minister' the top civil servants meet for lunch, drinks, dinner – see under Lynn & Jay in Chapter II.

Beefsteak Club, Irving Street, 1876 – followed on from the Beef-Steak Society, 1735-1867, which was not really a Club and met in various premises (latterly called the Sublime Society of Beef-Steaks). All the club waiters were/are supposedly called Charles.

Boodle's, St James's Street, 1762 – originally on Pall Mall, moving in 1783. Established by Edward Boodle as a proprietary club using premises owned by William Almack; the members acquired the building in 1896 from the then proprietor. Famous members include Beau Brummell and Edward Gibbon.

Brooks's Club, St James's Street, 1764 – originally on Pall Mall, moving in 1778: then a gambling and Whig haunt – Charles James Fox supposedly had to borrow from the waiters. Brooks's absorbed the Dilettanti Society, an C18 dining-society which had lived at the St James's Club from 1922, when the latter in 1975 was merged into Brooks's. Houses 'The Club' for its monthly dinners (see Grant Duff, 1905, for its history, 1764-1905). Established as another proprietor club by William Almack; then managed by William Brooks. Horace Walpole said that within the Club 'a thousand meadows and cornfields are staked at every throw' (as its noble wealthy landowning members gambled into the night).

Buck's Club, Clifford Street, 1919 – gave the world, or at least introduced the English to, 'Buck's Fizz'. Named after one of its founding members, Herbert Buckmaster.

Caledonian Club, Halkin Street, 1891.

Canning Club, St James's Square, 1911 (used to be the Argentine Club).

Carlton Club, St James's Street, 1832 – moved around before settling in the current premises by 1854; Members are still expected to be sympathetic to the Conservative Party, hence it being targeted by an IRA bomb in 1990. Lord Wemys was a member for 74 years until his death in 1914.

Cavalry and Guards Club, Piccadilly, 1890 – a military club as the name hints; the Cavalry Club (1890-1980s) was initially a proprietary club before becoming a members' club in 1895; amalgamated with the Guards Club (1810s) in 1976.

East India, Devonshire, Sports and Public Schools Club, St James's Street – Our Club with the longest name? Made up of the East India United Service Club, 1849, merging with the Sports Club in 1938 and then the Public Schools club in 1972 followed by the Devonshire Club in 1976. And the most merged of our Clubs?

Eccentric Club – see Savile Club.

Farmers Club, Whitehall Court, 1842.

Flyfishers' Club – see Savile Club.

Garrick Club, Garrick Street, 1831 – named after David Garrick, actor; for arty and media folk. Members include Dickens, Thackeray, Irving. No female members. (Not, of course, strictly within the boundaries of Clubland.)

Lansdowne Club, Fitzmaurice Place, 1935 – a sporty club, with a huge swimming-pool.

National Liberal Club, Whitehall Place, 1882 – the Club has Gladstone's 'Gladstone bag' and his famous axe for felling trees at Hawarden. Houses the Authors' Club, 1891; also the Savage Club as below.

Naval and Military Club, St James's Square, 1862 – aka the 'In and Out' after its one-time C19 Piccadilly premises with marked gateposts; in its fourth/current set of premises from 1999. Our most moved Club? Accommodates the Den Norske Klub, 1887.

(New Cavendish Club, Great Cumberland Place, 1920 – closed 2015!)

Oriental Club, Stratford Place, 1824 – originally for officers of the East India Company who were not eligible to join the other military clubs.

Portland Club, Pall Mall, 1816 (as the Stratford Club) – the home of bridge; now accommodated in the Savile Club.

Pratt's Club, Park Place, 1841 – our tiniest Club? Named after William Pratt, owner of 14 Park Place and Steward to the Duke of Beaufort; its servants, now staff, were/are all called George.

Reform Club, Pall Mall, 1836 – once the radicals' Club; Jules Verne had Phineas Fogg in its smoking-room take on the bet about 80 days to circumnavigate the globe (see Chapter II). Built by Charles Barry; Alexis Soyer as its famous chef – as discussed in Chapter IV.

Appendix

Royal Air Force Club, Piccadilly, 1918 – in the premises of the former Lyceum Club, bought with a gift of £100k from Lord Cowdray.

Royal Automobile Club, Pall Mall, 1897 – Burgess and Maclean lunched here before fleeing to Russia. Our largest Club in terms of membership at c13,500?

Royal Ocean Racing Club, St James's Place, 1925.

Royal Over-Seas League, St James's Street, 1910.

Savage Club, Whitehall Place, 1857 – named after the dissolute poet, Richard Swift; has moved around a great deal, now (back) sharing with the National Liberal Club above.

Savile Club, Brook Street, 1868 (initially as the New Club) – current premises from 1927. Accommodates the Eccentric Club (1781), the Flyfishers' Club (1884), and the Portland Club as above.

Travellers Club, Pall Mall, 1819 – built by Charles Barry for £64k; bombed 1940 and restored 1952/53.

Turf Club, Carlton House Terrace, 1861 – once known as the Arlington Club. Members 'cut' Churchill in the 1900s when he deserted the Tories for the Liberals – gossip that made the 'Washington Post'; and its Tory servants waited on him 'with evident disinclination'.

United Oxford and Cambridge Club, Pall Mall, formed in 1971 by the amalgamation of the Oxford and Cambridge University Club (1830) and the United University Club (1921) – the latter having merged with the New University Club (1868) in 1938. Now known as the Oxford and Cambridge Club, it possesses, fittingly, one of the largest libraries in Clubland. Although there is no obvious tension, at present, between the dark blues and the light blues as members of the 'United' Club, the two venerable ancient universities were really rather different historically – Oxford is the Humanities dominated institution, and was the Tory-Royalist supporter; while Cambridge is Science focussed, and was Whig-Parliamentarian (Brockliss, 2016). To this day, my 2017/18 University of Oxford dark-blue pocket diary finds the need usefully to remind me on 30th January: 'Charles I, King and Martyr'.

White's, St James's Street, 1736 - said to be the oldest and grandest Club in Clubland (perhaps the Establishment's club?). Linked to White's Chocolate House (1693) as established by Francis White (who makes it into the *DNB* – unlike Messrs Boodle and Brooks); and becoming a Club proper by the 1730s, a few decades ahead of Boodle's and Brooks's as above. After White died in 1711 the business was run by his widow and then from 1729 by their assistant, John Arthur. The shift to the present premises in 1787-88 also saw it become the favoured club for the Tories, while Brooks's soaked up the Whigs (the Tories later colonised the Carlton) – but gambling featured more than politics at both (but, interestingly, not smoking at White's until 1845 when a smoking-room was created). The bow-window was added in 1811, as famously promptly occupied by Beau Brummel. The members were not able to buy their Clubhouse until 1927, being outbid when it earlier came on the market and it was bought and run by a series owners as a proprietor club. Girtin (1964, p 18) quotes Disraeli (not a member) on Whites's: membership is 'a supreme human distinction comparable only to the Garter'.

And some other clubs, albeit not in Clubland proper: Chelsea Arts Club, Old Church Street, 1891; the City Livery Club, Upper Thames Street, 1914; the City of London Club, Old Broad Street, 1832; the City University Club, Cornhill, 1895; the Civil Service Club, Great Scotland Yard, 1953; the Alpine Club, Shoreditch, 1857; the London

Sketch Club, Chelsea, 1898; the MCC, 1781; the Queen's Club, West Kensington, 1886; the Roehampton Club, 1901; the Royal Thames Yacht Club, Knightsbridge, 1775; the Groucho Club, Dean Street, 1985 (Patten, 2015); the Hurlingham Club, Ranelagh Gardens, 1869; the London Press Club, Adam Street, 1882; the Special Forces Club, Knightsbridge, 1945; the Walbrook Club, 2000; the Civil Service Club, 1953; the University Women's Club, 1883; the Navel Club, 1946; the Fox Club (2003); the Sloan Club (1976).

The Institute of Directors, Pall Mall, 1903 – if this counts as a Club rather than a trade-body; but there was once the Number Ten Club, Belgrave Square, 1955-75, as a club for the IoD members, which was closed after amassing large debts, presumably lacking sound direction...

There is an Association of London Clubs as an umbrella 'trade' body to which most of the above belong.

C. Clubs New

A new wave of chic London clubs has emerged in recent years for an affluent younger generation, such as the 'Devonshire Square Club' and 'Mark's Club' as well as '12 Hay Hill', the 'Fox Club', '15 Hertford Street', 'The Hospital Club', 'The Clubhouse', 'Grace Belgravia', 'Little House', 'Home House', and 'Home Grown' (reputedly with a £2000 pa membership fee and an expected 3000 members). In 2016 '67 Pall Mall' opened as a wine club. There is also notably 'Soho House' (1995, as founded by Nick Jones), a rapidly expanding international chain of 15 or so locations (in 2016) globally (including a retreat in the Cotswolds – Soho Farmhouse at Great Tew) catering to over 50,000 members (with 30,000 or more on a waiting-list), and with a turn-over of about £300m (the *Financial Times* (2/4/16): 'a luxury brand synonymous with style celebrity') . And indeed Soho House now has a lifestyle guide on the 'Soho House Way', offering recipes, décor tips, design ideas – 'Eat Drink Nap: Bringing the House Home' (2014). Soho House has reportedly just spent £200m (sic) transforming a 1924 Lutyens Grade 1 Listed landmark building at No. 27 Poultry, City of London, that was once the HQ of the Midland Bank (*Financial Times*, 15/4/17): 'The Ned' (after Sir Edward Lutyens) will provide private club space but also be partially open to the public. These new private/commercial clubs echo the entrepreneurial proprietor clubs of the eighteenth-century discussed in Chapter I - rather than the unincorporated associations of the nineteenth-century creations using the legal and organisational model explored in Chapter III - but their networking function reflects that of the 'information hub' and social status driven expansion of Our Clubs in the later decades of the nineteenth-century as noted in Chapter I. As discussed above, if (rightly) Francis White got into the *DNB* for (almost) creating the proprietor club some two centuries ago, one may well wonder whether Nick Jones will enter the new *ODNB* for re-inventing the proprietary model in the 1990s.

These new Clubs are clearly responding to a very different market to that served in 2015 by Our Clubs: as Sathnam Sanghera put it in the *Times* (8/4/16), 'London is seeing the opening of a host of new co-working clubs that in no way resemble the gentlemen's clubs of old, where you had to dress up as if going to work but, paradoxically, were not allowed to take pen or paper or answer a phone.' – indeed, there is little resemblance since it seems a tad unlikely that, say, 'a nail bar and Botox services' will ever be available in such as the Athenaeum or the Reform! These are places where he saw 'attractive people networking with one another on expensive sofas in between important phone calls' (well, Our Clubs have the sofas) – and he quotes from the website of the very new 'Soho Works' offering 'an international network of round-the-clock workspaces designed and equipped to support a membership of individuals and businesses in the creative industries' (there is also 'The Ministry', an off-shoot of 'The Ministry of Sound' record label and nightclub, over at London Bridge which offers over 800 'fixed desks'). A new private members' club will be opened in the deprived area (in clubbery terms) of Kensington & Chelsea – 'Albert's'; with, according to the *FT* (9/8/16), an annual fee of £500 'and a tartan staircase'. The *FT* refers to estimates of there now being around 100 clubs in London, 'down from 180 in the 1880s [peak]' but up from the 1970s trough.

This new generation of clubs get glossy features in the press: the *Times Magazine* had 'Do you want to be in my club?' – noting that despite their 'vetting committees, waiting lists, hefty fees' clearly 'London's private club scene is booming' (it goes on to look at, inter alia, the revamping of Annabels, at the growth of Soho House, at the Curtain in Shoreditch, at '5 Hertford Street' in Mayfair). These places 'for the super-rich and business classes' are contrasted with

Our Clubs – 'once a club meant a grand building on Pall Mall, claret and stodgy boarding-school food'… Another feature in the *FT* magazine section was titled 'Meet, drink and be merry' in 'a new breed of members' club', focussing on Soho House and its 'Ned' building referred to above: the Ned has 1500 'founder members' (at £2500 pa), a 252-room hotel, a rooftop pool, a gym, a bar in the Bank's vault with its '20-tonne door', a 'banking hall' for '1,000 diners' and nine other 'eateries', etc, etc. The same article also mentions the Devonshire Club, the Curtain, and the Ten Trinity Square Private Club.

And John Gapper (*FT*, p 11, 8/2/18) reviews the success of Soho House and similar, wondering whether (in the context of SH's $2b NYSE float of its by then 18 sites with 70,000 members) being too open to new members risks over-crowding when Clubs usually thrive long-term 'on a sense of exclusivity – the urge to slip past the velvet rope and join an elite gathering' (to enter via a grand doorway on Pall Mall into an imposing edifice without any name-plate while passers-by wonder what that place is). And the *FT* (24/2/18, Emma Jacobs) featured 'All-female club aims to open doors for women' – 'All Bright' is a new 2018 business club for women near Oxford Street, quoting one of its founders when challenged as to whether the Club in offering blow-dries and yoga sessions might be pandering to stereotypes: 'You can be a feminist and still enjoy a blow-dry and yoga.'.

The fascination of the *FT* with such clubs continues: 'Members' clubs move with the times' (12/1/19) reports that 'Annabel's' has been revamped at a cost of at least £65m, and supposedly in the process has weeded out former members 'who are not really cool' and yet is still ending up with a waiting-list of 'about 4,500' – although one member is quoted as declaring that the membership is now 'very Eurotrash' compared, she says, to 5 Hertford and Soho House.

I need hardly add that your donnish author has never set foot in any of these exciting 'new generation' London clubs, being far too old and dull to be at all welcome – even if I knew anybody who might invite me in. I can only peer in and wonder if the world is now run from inside such places – like the excluded poor looking at the chandeliers in the windows of the Pall Mall clubs and asking if that is whence the Establishment runs the country. I have, however, called in at 'Mollie's' for a bacon butty since it is on my way to work: it is the first of an American-style motel and diner as part of the ever-expanding Soho House empire (on the Swindon-Oxford A420 near Buckland, and the breakfasts are indeed recommended!).

D. Clubs Fictional

See Chapter II for the Diogenes Club frequented by Mycroft Holmes and the Drones Club by Bertie Wooster. Others include (some also mentioned in Chapter II): the Beargarden Club in Trollope's 'Palliser' novels; the Bellona Club used by Lord Peter Wimsey in Dorothy Sayers' 'The Unpleasantness at the Bellona Club' – in addition, LPW was a member of the Egotist's Club; Blades Club as M's club in Flemings' James Bond novels; Featherstonehaugh's Club in the novel 'Clubbed to Death' by Ruth Dudley Edwards (the new-broom Club Secretary is found beneath the Gallery in the Saloon – did he fall or was he pushed? And the reforming Chairman of the Management Committee is later blown-up!); the Hotch Potch Club and also the Iseeum Club from Galsworthy's 'The Forsyte Saga'; the Junior Ganymede Club for Jeeves and fellow gentlemen's gentlemen; the Senior Conservative Club in Wodehouse's 'Psmith in the City'; the Mausoleum Club in Dennis Wheatley's 'Three Inquisitive People'; Brat's (Buck's) in Evelyn Waugh's 'A Handful of Dust'; and the Imperial Club from the 1960s sitcom series of over 100 episodes of 'Bootsie and Snudge' starring Alfie Bass and Bill Fraser (see Chapter II) – one is the Club's put-upon dogsbody and the other is the lordly Hall Porter (the series followed on from 'The Army Game'). A club 'factional' novel is Wintle (1961), 'The Club'.

E. Clubs New York

Beyond Our Clubs in London perhaps the next largest cluster of similar clubs is in New York. In the *FT Weekend Magazine* (15/12/18, 'Welcome to the Club') a new book of photographs of NY clubs is featured. Two still reject women; fees can reach $5k pa;

Appendix

they include: the Explorer, 1904; the Knickerbocker, 1871 (men only, and members have included Alexander Hamilton, Douglas Fairbanks, JP Morgan, Franklin D. Roosevelt); the Union League, 1863 (which possesses a collection of 14,000 toy soldiers); the Metropolitan, 1891 (members have included Nixon, Reagan, Ford, Clinton; it cost $57m to build in 2018 prices; and was almost bankrupt by the 1970s); the Cosmopolitan, 1909 (female only); Yale, 1897; and the Leash, 1925.

F. Clubs Provincial

From 'Whittaker's 2018' (pp 576/577) – the Athenaeum, Liverpool (1797); the New Club, Edinburgh (1787); the New Club, Cheltenham (1874); the Norfolk Club, Norwich (1770); the Northern Counties Club, Newcastle (1829); the Royal Northern and University Club, Aberdeen (1854); the Scottish Arts Club, Edinburgh (1872); the Ulster Reform Club, Belfast (1885); Vincent's, Oxford (1863), the Western Club, Glasgow (1825). And the Clifton Club, Bristol – albeit not listed in 'Whittaker's.

Bibliography

All these items will be found in a combination of the British Library, the Bodleian Library, the London Library, and the Guildhall Library – some Club libraries may have many of them. Most of the older texts on Our Clubs and Clubland can easily be obtained secondhand or as reprints from Amazon, and some are available free in digitalised form. This List does not pretend to show all the very many histories of individual Clubs. It does, however, seek to capture all the more general texts on Clubs, Clubland, and Clubbery.

'OUP' below is Oxford University Press

Ackroyd, P. (2016) *The History of England (Volume IV)* (Macmillan)

Addison, P. (2005) *Churchill: The Unexpected Hero* (OUP)

Allen, R.J. (1933) *The Clubs of Augustan London* (Harvard University Press)

Anderson, G. (1993) *Hang Your Halo in the Hall: History of the Savile Club* (Savile Club)

Annan, N. (1990) *Our Age: The Generation that Made Post-War Britain* (Weidenfeld & Nicolson)

Ashton, G. (2002) *Pictures in the Garrick Club* (Garrick Club)

Athenaeum, The (1975) *The Athenaeum: Club and Social Life in London, 1824-1974* (Heinemann)

Bibliography

Barnett, C. (1995) *The Lost Victory: British Dreams, British Realities* (Macmillan)

Bew, J. (2016) *Citizen Clem* (riverrun)

Bingham, T. (2010) *Dr Johnson and the Law: and other essays on Johnson* (Inner Temple and Dr Johnson's House)

Black, B. (2012) *A Room of His Own: A Literary-Cultural Study of Victorian Clubland* (Ohio University Press)

Blackham, R.J. (1931) *The Soul of the City: London's Livery Companies – Their Storied Past, Their Living Present* (Sampson Low, Marston & Co)

Blackham, R.J. (1932) *Wig and Gown: The Story of the Temple, Gray's and Lincoln's Inn* (Sampson Low, Marston & Co)

Blake, R. (1966) *Disraeli* (Methuen)

Bradley, S. (2015) *The Railways: Nation, Network and People* (Profile Books)

Brendon, P. (1997) *The Motoring Century: A History of the Royal Automobile Club* (Bloomsbury)

Breward, C. (2016) *The Suit: Form, Function and Style* (Reaktion Books)

Brewer, J. (1997) *Pleasures of the Imagination: English Culture in the Eighteenth-Century* (HarperCollins)

Brockliss, L.W.B. (2016) *The University of Oxford: A History* (OUP)

Burford, E.J. (1988) *Royal St James's: Being a Story of King's, Clubmen and Courtesans* (Hale)

Burrows, A. (2007) *English Private Law* (OUP)

Cannadine, D. (2017) *Victorious Century: The United Kingdom, 1800-1906* (Allen Lane, Penguin)

Cartoon Museum (2009) *A Peep into Clubland: Cartoons from Private London Clubs* (Cartoon Museum)

Cesarani, D. (2016), *Disraeli: The Novel Politician* (Yale University Press)

Clark, G. (1956) *The Later Stuarts, 1660-1714* (OUP)

Clark, P. (2000) *British Clubs and Societies, 1580-1800* (OUP)

Cohn-Sherbok (2018) *London Clubs* (Kindle)

Coote, C.R. (1971) *The Other Club* (Sidgwick & Jackson)

Cowan, B. (2005) *The Social Life of Coffee: The Emergence of the British Coffeehouse* (Yale University Press)

Cowell, F.R. (1975) *The Athenaeum: Club and Social Life in London, 1824-1974* (Heinemann)

Darwin, B. (1943) *British Clubs* (Collins)

Davis, A. (2018) *Reckless opportunists: Elites at the end of the Establishment* (Manchester University Press)

DeSantis, A. (2007) *Inside Greek U: Fraternities, Sororities, and the Pursuit of Pleasure, Power, and Prestige* (The University of Kentucky Press)

Dixon, A.K. (2009) *The Army and Navy Club* (A&N Club)

Doughan, D. & Gordon, P. (2006) *Women, Clubs and Associations in Britain* (Routledge)

Eatwell, R. & Goodwin, M. (2018) *National Populism: The Revolt against Liberal Democracy* (Pelican/Penguin)

Ellis, W. (1994) *The Oxbridge Conspiracy: How the Ancient Universities kept their Stranglehold on the Establishment* (Michael Joseph)

Escott, T.H.S. (1914) *Club Makers and Club Members* (Fisher Unwin)

Farrington, D. & Palfreyman, D. (2012) *The Law of Higher Education* (OUP)

Fitzgerald, K. (1968) *Ahead of Their Time: A Short History of the Farmers' Club* (Heinemann)

Fleming, R. (2010) *Britain after Rome: The Fall and Rise, 400 to 1070* (Penguin)

Forrest, D. (1968, 1979) *The Oriental: Life Story of a West End Club* (Batsford)

Fulford, R. (1962) *Boodle's: A Short History* (Boodle's)

Gatrell, V. (2006) *City of Laughter: Sex and Satire in Eighteenth-Century London* (Atlantic Books)

Gilliver, P. (2016) *The Making of the Oxford English Dictionary* (OUP)

Girouard, M. (1990) *The English Town* (Yale University Press)

Girtin, T. (1964) *The Abominable Clubman* (Hutchinson)

Graham, A. (1957) *The Club: A Novel* (Macmillan)

Grant, W. (2000) *Pressure Groups and British Politics* (Macmillan)

Grant Duff, M.E. (1905) *The Club, 1764-1905* (Privately Printed)

Graves, C. (1963) *Leather Armchairs: The Chivas Regal book of London Clubs* (Cassell) – and a 1964 edition as *Leather Armchairs: The Book of London Clubs*

Greig, H. (2013) *The Beau Monde: Fashionable Society in Georgian London* (Oxford University Press)

Griffiths, A.G.F. (1907) *Clubs and Clubmen* (Hutchinson)

Guedalla, P. (1926) *Palmerston* (Billing & Sons)

Guttsman, W.L. (1963) *The British Political Elite* (MacGibbon & Kee)

Harrison, B. (2009) *Seeking a Role – The United Kingdom, 1951-1970* (OUP)

Harrison, B. (2010) *Finding a Role? – The United Kingdom, 1970-1990* (OUP)

Harrison, C.E. (1999) *The Bourgeois Citizen in Nineteenth-Century France: Gender, Sociability, and the Uses of Emulation* (OUP)

Hatton, J. (1890) *Clubland: London and Provincial* (JS Virtue & Co)

Hitchins, H. (2005) *Dr Johnson's Dictionary: The Extraordinary Story of the Book that defined the World* (John Murray)

Hoppit, J. (2000) *A Land of Liberty? – England, 1689-1727* (OUP)

Hough, R.A. (1986) *The Ace of Clubs: A History of the Garrick* (Andre Deutsch)

Hughes, S.L. (1912) *The English Character* (T.N. Foulis)

Bibliography

Hunt, T. (2009) *The Frock-Coated Communist: The Life and Times of the Original Champagne Socialist* (Penguin)

Ingamells, J. (2013) *Brooks's, 1764-2014: The Story of a Whig Editor* (Paul Holberton Publishing)

Ivey, G.J. (1880) *Clubs of the World: A General Guide or Index to the London & Country Clubs and those of...* (Harrison)

Kaufman, J. (2002) *For the Common Good? – American Civic Life and the Golden Age of Fraternity* (OUP)

Jacoby, C. (2009) *The East India Club: A History* (East India Club)

Jones, L.C. (1942) *The Clubs of the Georgian Rakes* (Columbia University Press)

Jones, O. (2015) *The Establishment: And How They Get Away With It* (Penguin)

Kay, O. de (1994) *From the Age that is Past: Harvard Club of New York City* (HC of NYC)

Kendall, D. (2008) *Members Only: Elite Clubs and the Process of Exclusion* (Rowan & Littlefield)

King, A. (2015) *Who Governs Britain?* (Pelican)

Kishlansky, M. (1996) *A Monarchy Transformed: Britain 1603-1714* (Penguin)

Klimczuk, S. & Warner, G. (2009) *Secret Places, Hidden Sanctuaries* (Sterling Ethos)

Kinnear, A. (1902) *London Clubs* ('Munsey's Magazine')

Lane Fox, R. (2005) *The Classical World: An Epic History from Homer to Hadrian* (Allen Lane, Penquin)

Langford, P. (1989) *A Polite and Commercial People – England, 1727-1783* (OUP)

Lejeune, A. (1979, 1984, 1997) *The Gentlemen's Clubs of London* (Parkgate Books)

Lejeune, A. (2012) *The Gentlemen's Clubs of London* (Stacey International)

Lejeune, A. (1993) *White's: The First Three Hundred Years* (Black)

Letts, Q. (2017) *Patronising Bastards: How the elites betrayed Britain* (Constable)

Lord, E. (2008) *The Hell-Fire Clubs: Sex, Satanism and Secret Societies* (Yale University Press)

Lutz, D. (2011) *Pleasure Bound: Victorian Sex Rebels and the New Eroticism* (W.W. Norton)

McDouall, R. (1974) *Clubland Cooking* (Phaidon)

Machray, R. (1902) *The Night Side of London* (Unknown)

Magnus, P. (1954) *Gladstone* (Murray)

Marsh, C. (1828) *The Clubs of London: With anecdotes of their members, sketches of character, and conversations* (Colburn) – NB The British Library Catalogue has the author as Colin Mackenzie rather than Charles Marsh, and, adding to the confusion, a book of the same title, year, publisher is shown under R. Brinsley Sheridan...

Marshall, C. McDonald (2014) *Recipes from the Reform: A Selection of Recipes from the Reform Club, London* (The Reform Club)

Marwick, A. (1998) *The Sixties* (OUP)

Mills, C. Wright (1956) *The Power Elite* (OUP)

Milne-Smith, A. (2011) *London Clubland: A Cultural History of Gender and Class in Late Victorian Britain* (Palgrave Macmillan)

Moers, E. (1960) *The Dandy: Brummell to Beerbohm* (Secker & Warburg)

More, K.M. (1908) *Despatches from Ladies' Clubland* (K. Mervin More)

Nevill, R. (1911) *London Clubs: Their History & Treasures* (Chatto & Windus)

Newark, T. (2015) *The In & Out: A History of the Navel and Military Club* (Osprey)

O'Connor, A. (1976) *Clubland: The Wrong Side of the Right People* (Martin Brian & O'Keeffe)

Palfreyman, D. (2008) *The Oxford Tutorial* (OxCHEPS – and at the Occasional Papers page of the OxCHEPS website)

Palfreyman, D. (2010) *London's Livery Companies* (Oracle)

Palfreyman, D. (2011) *London's Inns of Court* (Oracle)

Palfreyman on 'The Law of Higher Education' (OUP, 2012) – see Farrington & Palfreyman.

Palfreyman, D. & Tapper, T. (2014) *Reshaping the University: The Rise of the Regulated Market in Higher Education* (OUP)

Palfreyman, D. & Temple, P. (2017) *Universities and Colleges: A Very Short Introduction* (OUP)

Palfreyman, D. (forthcoming) *London's Royal Societies, Institutions, and Colleges* (Amazon/Kindle)

Patten, A. (2015) *The Groucho Club: 30th Anniversary* (Preface Publishing)

Paxman, J. (1990) *Friends in High Places: Who Runs Britain?* (Penguin)

Perry, M. (2003) *The House in Berkeley Square: History of the Lansdowne Club* (Lansdowne Club)

Petrie, C. & Cooke, A. (2007) *Carlton Club, 1832-2007* (Carlton Club)

Picard, L. (2005) *Victorian London: The Life of a City, 1840-1870* (Weidenfeld & Nicolson)

Philippson, N. (2011) *Adam Smith: An Enlightened Life* (Penguin)

Plumb, J.H. (1950), *England in the Eighteenth Century (1714-1815)* (Pelican)

Porter, R. (1982) *English Society in the Eighteenth Century* (Pelican)

Porter, R. (1994) *London: A Social History* (Hamish Hamilton)

Probert, H. & Gilbert, M. (2004) *'128' The Story of the Royal Air Force Club* (RAF Club)

Putnam, R.D. (2000) *Bowling Alone: The collapse and revival of American community* (Simon & Schuster)

Robinson, J.M. (2018) *The Travellers Club: A Bicentennial History* (Libanus Press)

Ross, J.C. (1976) *An Assembly of Good Fellows: Voluntary associations in history* (Greenwood)

Sampson, A. (1962) 'The Mystique of British Clubs' in *Harper's Magazine* (November, p 42)

Sampson, A. (1962) *Anatomy of Britain* (Hodder and Stoughton)

Sampson, A. (1965) *Anatomy of Britain Today* (Hodder and Stoughton)

Sampson, A. (1971) *New Anatomy of Britain Today* (Hodder and Stoughton)

Sampson, A. (1982) *The Changing Anatomy of Britain* (Hodder and Stoughton)

Sampson, A. (1992) *The Essential Anatomy of Britain* (Hodder and Stoughton)

Sampson, A. (2004) *Who Runs This Place? – The Anatomy of Britain in the 21st Century* (John Murray)

Sandbrook, D. (2005) *Never Had It So Good: A History of Britain from Suez to the Beatles* (Abacus)

Sandbrook, D. (2010) *State of Emergency: The Way We Were – Britain, 1970-1974* (Penguin)

Sandbrook, D. (2015) *The Great British Dream Factory: The Strange History of Our National Imagination* (Allen Lane, Penguin)

Scott, J. (1991) *Who Rules Britain?* (Polity Press)

Scruton, R. (2006) *England: An Elergy* (Continuum)

Shenton, C. (2016), *Mr Barry's War: Rebuilding the Houses of Parliament after the Great Fire of 1834* (OUP)

Taddei, A. (1999) *London Clubs in the Late Nineteenth Century* (Discussion Papers in Economic and Social History: No. 28 (April 1998), University of Oxford)

Thevoz, S.A. (2018) *Club Government: How the Early Victorian World was Ruled from London Clubs* (I.B. Taurus)

Thomas, H. (ed) (1958) *The Establishment: A Symposium* (Anthony Blond)

Thole, J. (1992) *The Oxford and Cambridge Clubs in London* (The United Oxford and Cambridge Club)

Timbs, J. (1866) *Club Life of London* (Richard Bentley)

Tombs, R. (2014) *The English and their History* (Penguin)

Tosh, J. (1999, 2007) *A Man's Place: Masculinity and the Middle-Class Home in Victorian England* (Yale University Press)

Underwood, S. (1998) *A History of London* (Macmillan)

Vallance, E. (2009) *A Radical History of Britain* (Little, Brown)

Wansell, G. (2004) *The Garrick Club – A History* (Unicorn Press)

Ward, E. (1709) *The History of the London Clubs or the Citizens' Pastime by the Author of the London Spy* (Dutten)

Watson, J.S. (1960) *The Reign of George III, 1760-1815* (OUP)

Wiesner-Hanks, M.E. (2015) *A Concise History of THE WORLD* (Cambridge University Press)

Wilson, A.N. (2002) *The Victorians* (Hutchinson)

Wilson, A.N. (2005) *After the Victorians* (Hutchinson)

Winchester, S. (2003) *The Meaning of Everything: The Story of the Oxford English Dictionary* (OUP)

Wintle, A.D. (1961) *The Club* (Cassell)

Woodbridge, G. (1978) *The Reform Club, 1836-1978: A History from the Club's Records* (The Reform Club)

Ziegler, P. & S. Desmond (1991) *Brooks's: A Social History* (Constable)

Index

'Bootsie and Snudge', 44, 78, 79, 142
'Clubland', the journal, 44
'The Club', 27, 28, 31, 132, 142
'Bootsie & Snudge', 177
Almack's, 8, 24, 28, 45, 128
Annan, 48, 116, 118, 144
Assemblies, vi, 7
   Assembly Rooms, 13, 35
Athenaeum, 4, 11, 12, 15, 19, 26, 27, 28, 32, 37, 38, 45, 50, 52, 53, 54, 55, 57, 58, 60, 64, 65, 66, 70, 71, 72, 73, 91, 93, 94, 106, 110, 114, 117, 121, 124, 130, 132, 139, 143, 144, 146, 178, 179, 180, 181, 183, 208
Attlee, 58, 111, 126
Bachelor Problem, 37, 42
Bampton, 23, 81
Barry, 38, 79, 107, 134, 135, 154
Beast of Bolsover, 49
Beau Brummell, 30, 31, 132
Beau Nash, 13
Beerbohm, 31, 106, 151
Black-balling aka Pilling, 27, 28, 41, 45, 46, 63, 64, 76, 101, 125
Blackham, 4, 145
Blades, 50, 78, 130, 142
Blomfield, 107, 171, 172, 173, 174, 175, 176, 220
Bond
   James Bond, 50, 78, 142
Boodle's, 11, 19, 28, 30, 32, 36, 50, 52, 63, 72, 103, 110, 132, 136, 147, 189
Brexit, 122
Brooks's, 11, 19, 24, 26, 28, 30, 31, 32, 36, 52, 121, 129, 132, 136, 149, 155
Buck's, 28, 72, 77, 133, 142
Burton, 38, 106
Carlton, 19, 26, 27, 46, 70, 87, 108, 129, 133, 135, 136, 152
Cartoons in Clubs, 59, 106, 111
Cases in Club Law, 87
Churchill, 28, 135, 144
Club Carriages, 40

Index

Club Cuisine and Recipes, 102, 104, 121, 138, 207
Club Dandies, 8, 31, 73
Clubland, the area defined, i, 2, 8, 9, 11, 22, 47, 134, 136, 211, 212, 213
Coffee-houses, 2, 10, 13, 23, 24, 25, 29, 32, 35, 36, 104, 184, 185
Committees in Clubs, 18, 20, 40, 46, 54, 55, 60, 65, 66, 67, 68, 71, 82, 85, 86, 92, 94, 95, 97, 99, 101, 129
Cyberspace, Clubs in, 90, 125
Definitions of Club, 9, 42
Diogenes Club, 64, 67, 94, 142
Disraeli, 26, 27, 28, 59, 64, 136, 145, 146
Drones Club, 33, 77, 96, 142
Eccentrics, 38, 44
Encyclopaedia Britannica, 9
Establishment, i, 10, 23, 28, 32, 46, 47, 48, 49, 50, 52, 53, 54, 55, 56, 58, 60, 61, 62, 71, 111, 116, 117, 119, 121, 126, 136, 141, 146, 147, 149, 154
Expulsion, 87, 209
Garrick Club, 3, 119, 134, 144, 154
Gladstone, 26, 27, 28, 66, 134, 150
Groucho, 125, 137, 152
Hall Porter, 44, 46, 68, 79, 101, 113, 142, 182
Hastings, 70, 86, 119
Hellfire Clubs, 23, 31, 32, 163
Husbands, prospective & actual – hiding in Clubs, 39, 59, 73, 199
Imperial, 44, 79, 80, 90, 99, 142
Inns of Court, i, iv, 1, 2, 4, 17, 48, 81, 82, 83, 87, 106, 125, 151, 229
IoD, 137
JCRs, 81, 112, 113
Jeeves, 72, 142
Johnson, 7, 8, 9, 29, 30, 31, 79, 80, 121, 124, 130, 145, 148
Ladies' Clubs, 10, 12, 45, 59, 78
Lejeune, 5, 19, 106, 108, 109, 116, 150
Livery Companies, i, iv, 1, 2, 3, 4, 18, 49, 81, 83, 102, 106, 125, 145, 151, 228
Macaulay, 29
Maitland, 62, 81, 83, 84
Management Committee, 18, 91, 92, 94, 101, 142
Media, Clubs in the, 43, 44, 78, 120
Meistersinger, Die, 79
Nash, 13, 38
National Liberal, 52, 107, 110, 124, 134, 135

National Populism, 147
New York Clubs, 10, 16, 142
Newspapers, treatment of Clubs, 118, 119, 120, 121, 122, 123, 124, 138, 139, 140
Oxford & Cambridge Club, vi, 6, 171, 172, 173, 174, 175, 176
Palmerston, 27, 28, 148
Paxman, 31, 50, 51, 52, 54, 116, 152
Pepys, 9, 11, 32
Pooter, 39, 66
RAC, 19, 57, 88, 121
Reform Club, 39, 55, 60, 76, 78, 103, 107, 108, 122, 123, 134, 143, 150, 155
Rules, 18, 45, 80, 85, 86, 88, 89, 90, 92, 93, 105, 153
Sala, 14, 43, 44
Sampson, 49, 54, 55, 116, 117, 118, 145, 153
Savage, 14, 38, 43, 44, 114, 134, 135, 191
SCRs, 112, 114
Scruton, 16, 17, 153
Secretary/Secretaries – key role within Clubs, 20, 39, 51, 65, 67, 68, 71, 79, 94, 96, 97, 99, 101, 123, 142
Shaw, 8
Shuttleworth Port Railway, 115
Smirke, 107
Smith, Adam, 16
Soho House and the new chic clubs, 4, 117, 124, 125, 138, 139, 140, 142
Soyer, 102, 103, 134
Tombs, 22, 23, 34, 117, 154
Travellers, 27, 38, 54, 65, 66, 91, 96, 107, 130, 135, 152
Trollope, 3, 53, 59, 75, 117, 129, 132, 142, 229, 230
Trump, 124
Umbrellas, 69, 70
US Clubs, 10, 125
Walpole, 8, 23, 71, 133
Waterhouse, 107
White's, 11, 19, 24, 28, 30, 32, 36, 63, 64, 109, 111, 120, 129, 136, 150, 187, 190, 193
Wintle, Col., 69, 99, 224, 225, 226

A Compendium of Images

The Reader can locate a wealth of images of Clubs at their glitzy websites and also at Google Images under searches of Club names. Here I take the opportunity to reproduce old images used in books long out-of-print that the Reader may never otherwise see. This Compendium is for flipping through and I hope the images neatly link back to many of the themes explored in the main text.

JACOB TONSON
SECRETARY TO THE KIT-CAT CLUB
From a mezzotint by John Faber after the Kit-Cat portrait by Sir Godfrey Kneller

From Allen, R. (1933)

THE CALVES-HEAD CLUB

*The true Effigies of the Members of
The Calve's Head Club, Held on y*e* 30*th* of January 1734. at
y*e* Golden Eagle in Suffolk street in y*e* County
of MIDDLESEX.
From a satiric engraving in the Collection of Prints and
Drawings in the British Museum*

From Allen, R. (1933)

THE HELL-FIRE CLUB

The Diabolical Maskquerade,
Or the Dragon's-Feast as Acted by the HELL-FIRE-CLUB,
at Somerset House in the Strand.
From a satiric engraving in the Collection of Prints
and Drawings in the British Museum

From Allen, R. (1933)

A Compendium of Images

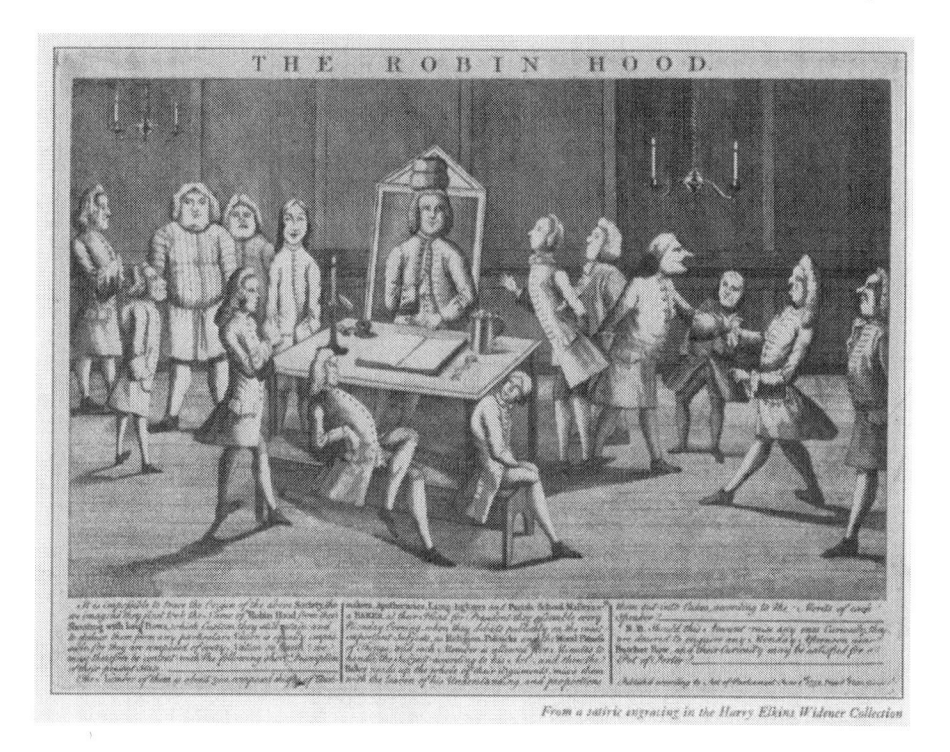

From Allen, R. (1933)

London's Pall Mall Clubs

MI5 — THE SECURITY SERVICE

Great assumptions about a career at MI5

No 1: Application by invitation only

No 2: You'll have to live your life undercover

No 3: You'll get a great company car

No 4: It's like a gentleman's club

Four advertisements from the MI5 2002–3 recruitment campaign, designed to help dispel myths about the Security Service and indicate that a sense of humour was part of Service culture.

From Andrew, C. (2009)

From Art of Dressing (1876)

DEDICATED

TO MY OLD AND *TRUSTY* FRIEND,

A. Taylor,

TO WHOM TO HIS *CREDIT* BE IT SAID;
I SHALL CONTINUE TO OWE
AN ETERNAL DEBT—OF GRATITUDE.

THE AUTHOR.

Megatherium Club, Pall Mall,
May 1876.

THE GENTLEMAN'S

ART OF DRESSING

WITH ECONOMY.

BY

A LOUNGER AT THE CLUBS.

T. W. DORÉ,
Court Tailor,

25 CONDUIT ST., AND 36 GEORGE ST.,
HANOVER SQUARE,

Uses none but the Best Materials, and keeps a Large Assortment of the Latest Novelties always in Stock. Every attention is paid to the wishes of the Customer, and *all Garments are cut and made by experienced Workmen*, careful regard being given to the prevailing Style, and the taste and requirements of the wearer.

Price List.

	£	s.	d.
Improved Ulster	3	3	0
Frock Coat	4	10	0
Vest	1	0	0
Trousers	1	8	0
Dress Coat	4	4	0
Do. Vest	1	1	0
Do. Trousers	1	15	0
Morning Coat	3	10	0
Do. Vest	0	15	0
Winter Overcoat	4	10	0
Summer do.	2	10	0
Suit of Dittos	4	4	0

The Livery Department continues to receive special attention, and Gentlemen who are particular as to the fit and style of their Servants' Clothes are respectfully solicited to favour it with a trial.

Terms: Five per Cent. Discount for Cash on delivery.

25 CONDUIT ST., AND 36 GEORGE ST.,
HANOVER SQUARE.

From Art of Dressing (1876)

A Compendium of Images

FIGURE 5.1. "Club Types" from *The Strand*, by Max Beerbohm, 1892.

From Black, B. (2014)

167

London's Pall Mall Clubs

2. CLUB TYPES

From Black, B. (2014)

A Compendium of Images

FIGURE E.3. "Husbands in Waiting," by Phil May. From *Punch's Almanack for 1897*.

From Black, B. (2014)

169

The United University Club, London.

Reginald Blomfield, A.R.A., Architect.

THE United University Club, Pall Mall, S.W., has been rebuilt on the old site and upon the same area as the old clubhouse. As the club accommodation had to be greatly increased, and bedrooms for members provided, the plan had to be carefully considered in order to comply with the conditions of the problem. The old club-house followed the usual practice of devoting the centre third of the building to a grand staircase, which took up a great deal of room and wasted more by separating the club into two halves. Such a plan was out of the question in the new building, and in order to provide the requisite accommodation it was necessary to place the hall and main staircase at the north end of the building facing west down Suffolk Place. This arrangement has the further advantage of opening up the entrance from the Haymarket along Suffolk Place.

The club-house contains, in the basement, kitchen and all offices and cellars; on the ground floor, smoking-room (west), reading-room (south), entrance-hall, main and back stairs, and lavatories; on the first floor are the club dining-rooms, *en suite* and occupying the whole of the fronts to Suffolk Street and Pall Mall, coffee-room, main and back stairs, lavatories, &c.; on the second floor, library, smoking library, billiard-room, card-room, secondary main stairs and back stairs, lavatories, &c.; on the third floor, billiard-room, card-room, three members' bedrooms, bath-rooms, lavatories, &c., and secondary main and back stairs; on the fourth floor, seven members' bed-

CHIMNEYPIECE IN DINING-ROOM.

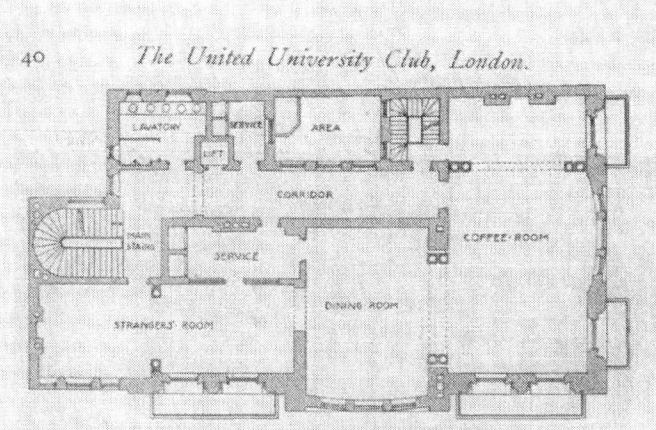

A Compendium of Images

40   *The United University Club, London.*

FIRST FLOOR PLAN

rooms, steward's room, and boy's bedroom, bathroom, etc., and secondary main and back stairs. A passenger lift runs up to third floor; a double-service lift from basement to fourth floor, with service-rooms on every floor, and double-service lifts from basement to dining-rooms on first floor.

The façades are faced with Portland stone, and the roof is covered with Westmorland slates. The building throughout is of fire-resisting construction. Messrs. Holloway Bros. were the general contractors. The enriched plaster-work throughout and all internal carving except billiard-room mantel were by Messrs. Geo. Jackson & Sons. The cooking installation by Messrs. James Slater & Co. The lifts by Messrs. Waygood. The electric lighting by Mr. A. W. Sclater, of Oxford Street, who also carried out the telephone system, electric bells, and speaking tubes. All internal plumbing, hot-water, and heating by Messrs. Matthew Hall & Co.; the wrought iron-work by Messrs. Elsley; and the whole of the external carving was executed by Messrs. Anmonier & Son, the figures in the frieze in Suffolk Street from models by Mr. Henry Pegram, A.R.A. The marble work was executed by J. Whitehead & Sons, Ltd. The whole of the work has been carried out from the designs and under the superintendence of the architect. Mr. A. B. Downs was clerk of the works.

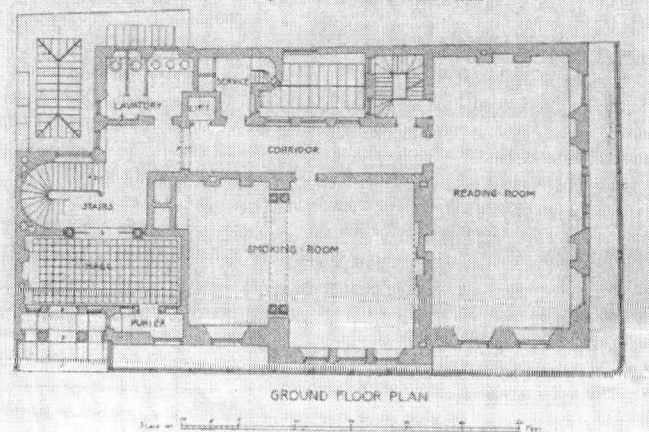

GROUND FLOOR PLAN

From Blomfield

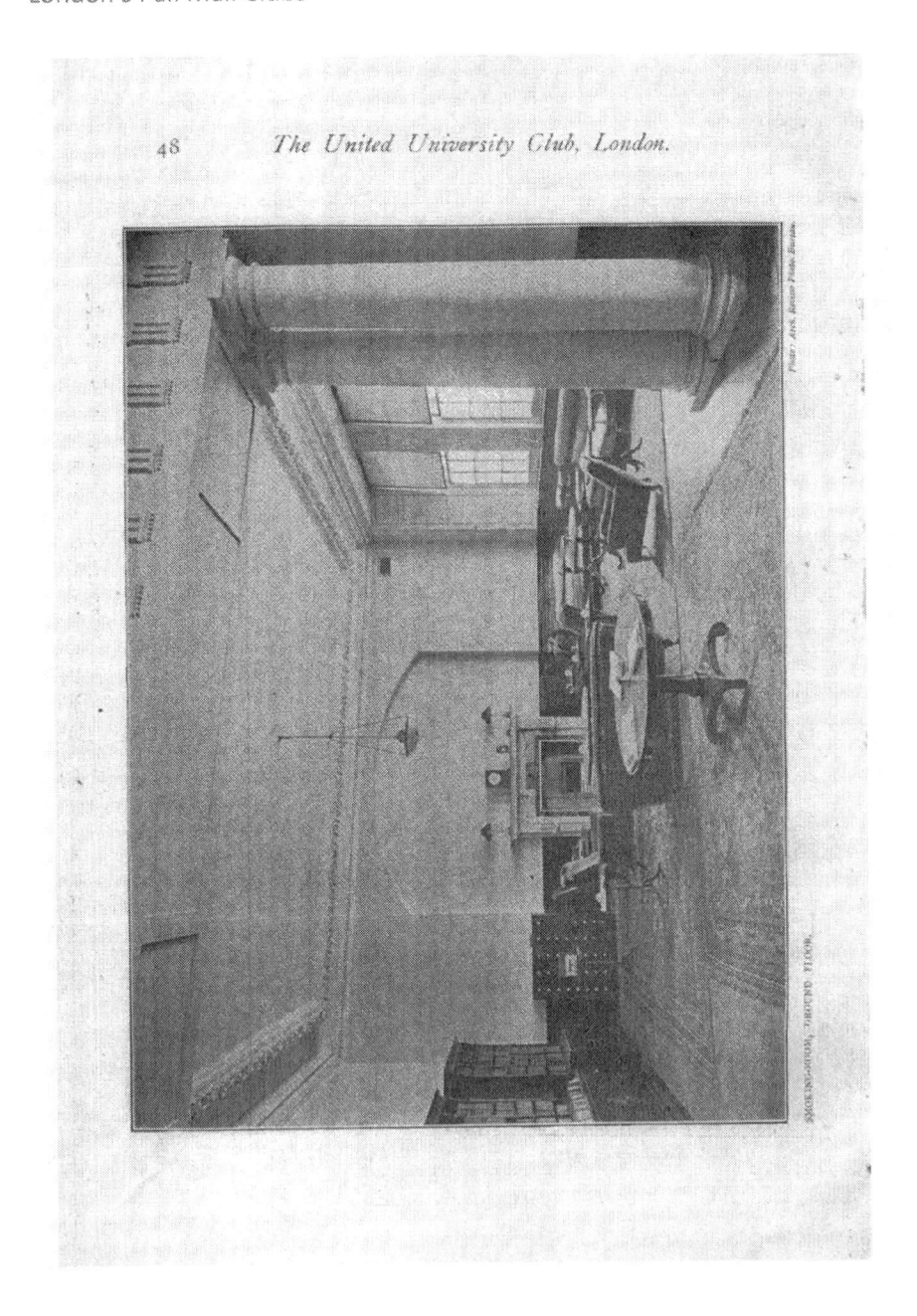

48 The United University Club, London.

From Blomfield

42   The United University Club, London.

THE OUTER HALL AND ENTRANCE DOOR.

From Blomfield

From Blomfield

A Compendium of Images

38   The United University Club, London.

GENERAL VIEW FROM PALL MALL EAST.

From Blomfield

London's Pall Mall Clubs

Bootsie and Snudge DVD

A Compendium of Images

John Wilson Croker, Founder of the Club, by Sir Francis Chantrey, R.A.

Decimus Burton, Architect of the Club House.

From Cowell, F.R. (1975) re the Athenaeum

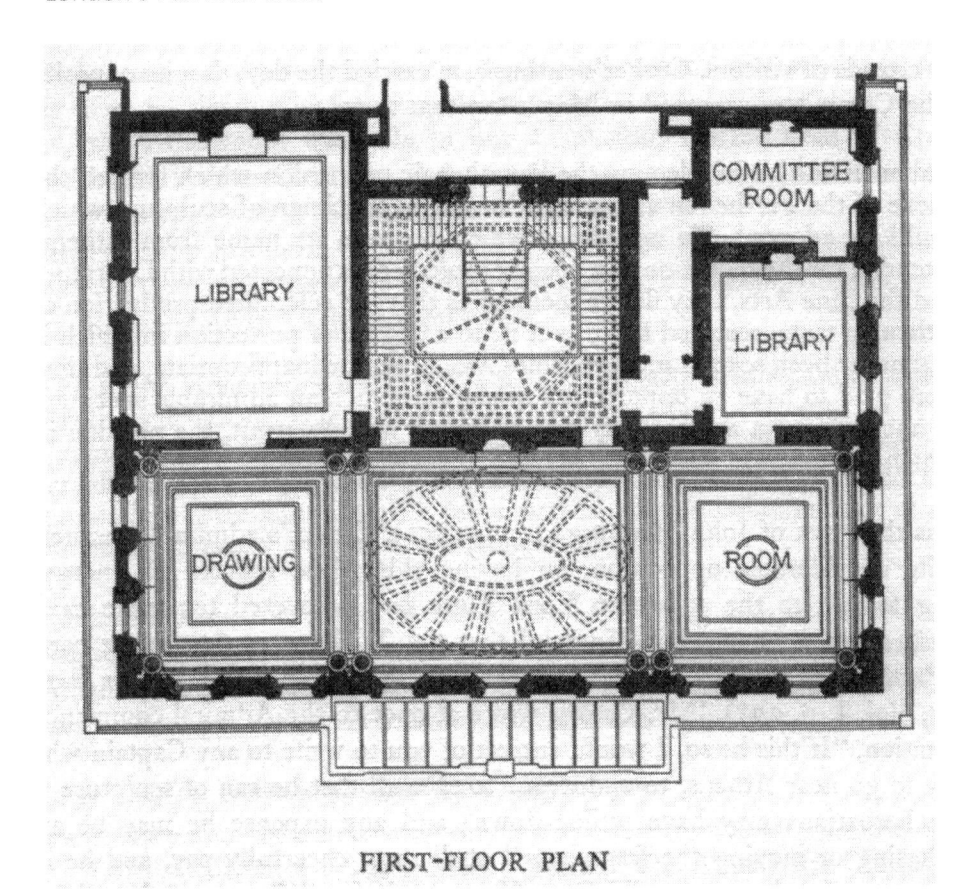

FIRST-FLOOR PLAN

From Cowell, F.R. (1975)

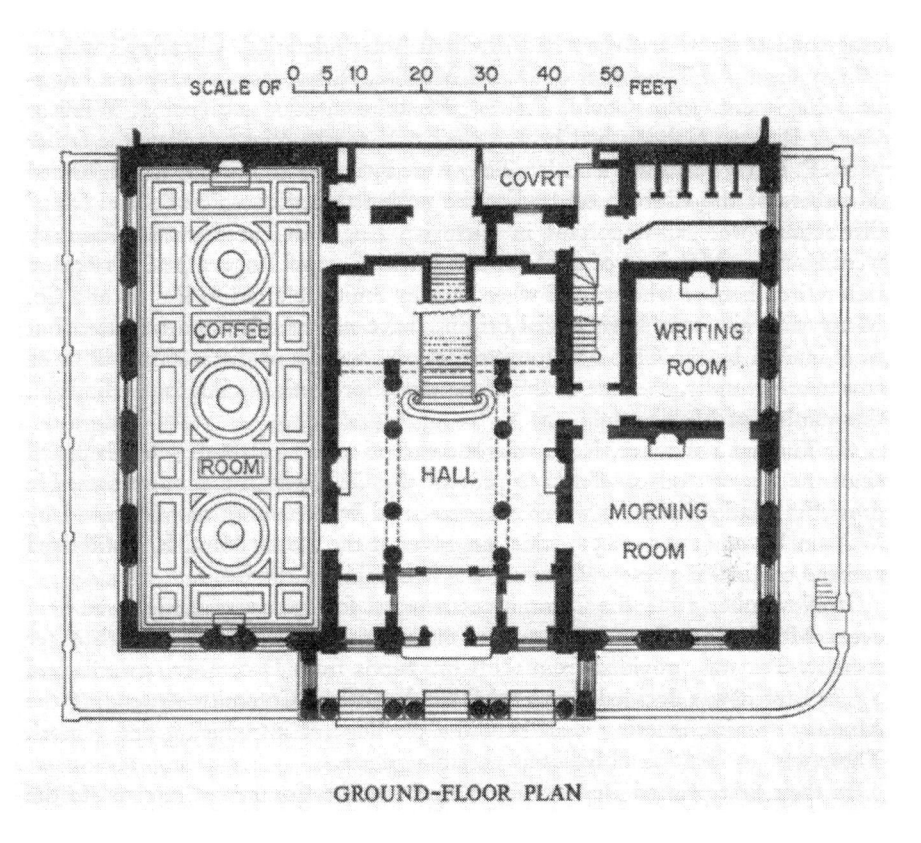

From Cowell, F.R. (1975)

London's Pall Mall Clubs

The Athenaeum before the addition of the Attic Storey.

Examples of Club Furniture dating from 1830–1840.

From Cowell, F.R. (1975)

A Compendium of Images

A Porter to the Hogarth Club
Pen and wash drawing by W. Holman Hunt, 1827-1910

From Darwin, B. (1943)

London's Pall Mall Clubs

THE HALL OF THE ATHENAEUM
Nineteenth century engraving by W. Taylor after J. Holland

From Darwin, B. (1943)

A Compendium of Images

LLOYD'S COFFEE HOUSE, LONDON
Coloured aquatint by William Holland, 1798

From Darwin, B. (1943)

183

London's Pall Mall Clubs

INTERIOR OF WHITE'S CHOCOLATE HOUSE, BEFORE 1733
Gaming House Scene from *The Rake's Progress*
Engraving by William Hogarth

From Darwin, B. (1943)

184

A Compendium of Images

THE CALVES HEAD CLUB
Pencil and wash drawing by William Hogarth, 1734

From Darwin, B. (1943)

Going to WHITES.

From Darwin, B. (1943)

TO

Sir EDWARD LETCHWORTH, F.S.A.

THE GRAND SECRETARY OF FREEMASONS,
HIMSELF A CLUBMAN OF THE BEST TYPE: ONE O
THE OLDEST AS WELL AS THE MOST VALUED AMONG
THOSE FOR WHOSE FRIENDSHIP THE PRESENT WRITER IS INDEBTED
TO A CLUB LIFE OF MORE THAN HALF A CENTURY.
IN GRATEFUL MEMORY OF
A COURTESY THAT NOTHING COULD RUFFLE,
OF AN AMIABILITY THAT NOTHING COULD ALIENATE,
AND OF KINDLY OFFICES SUSPENDED BY NO VICISSITUDES,
THIS VOLUME IS INSCRIBED BY HIS
GRATEFUL AND ATTACHED
T. H. S. ESCOTT.

From Escott, T. (1914)

London's Pall Mall Clubs

BOODLE'S CLUB : THE BAY WINDOW.

From Escott, T. (1914)

A PAGE FROM WHITE'S BETTING BOOK.
(By permission of the Club.)

From Escott, T. (1914)

London's Pall Mall Clubs

"SAVAGE CLUB WELCOME

SAVAGE CLUB HOUSE DINNER
SATURDAY APRIL 12TH 1902
DR PHINEAS S. ABRAHAM IN THE CHAIR.

AN IRVING NIGHT AT THE SAVAGE CLUB.
By W. H. Pike, R.B.A.
(By permission of the Club.)

From Escott, T. (1914)

A Compendium of Images

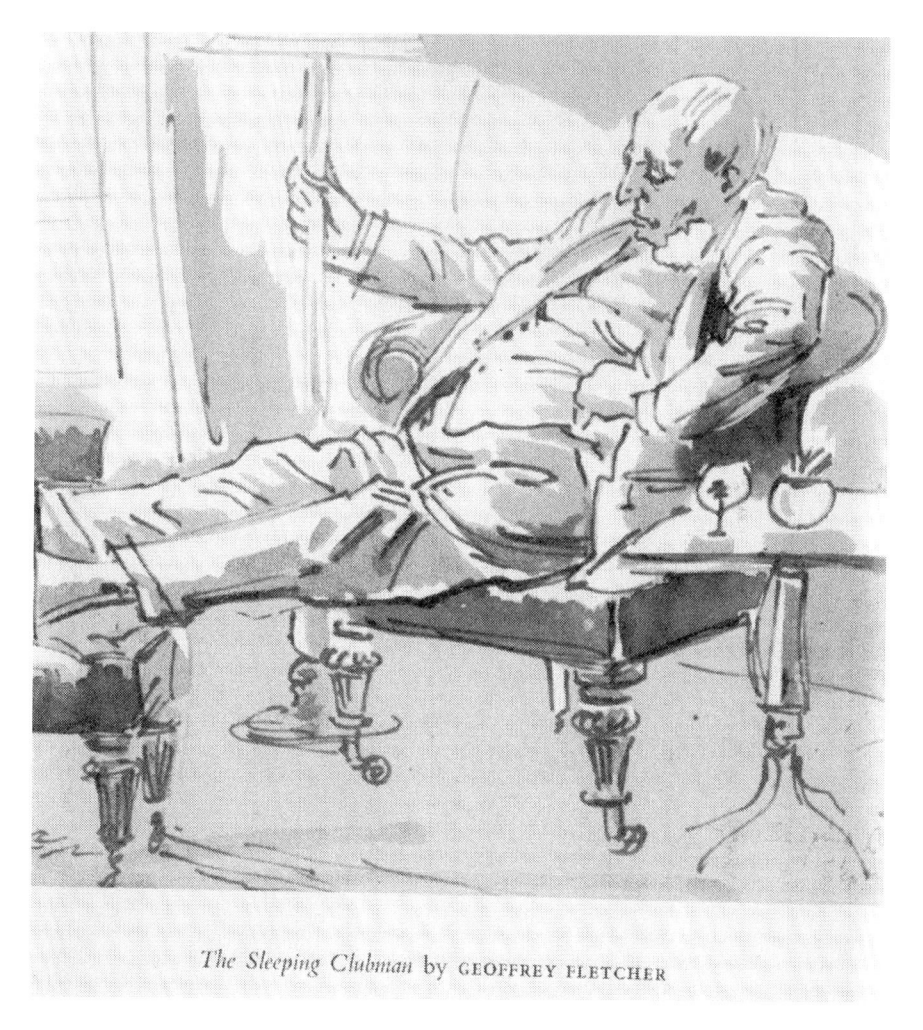

The Sleeping Clubman by GEOFFREY FLETCHER

From Girtin, T. (1964)

THE STAIRCASE, WHITE'S

From Graves, C. (1963)

A Compendium of Images

THE COFFEE ROOM, NAVAL AND MILITARY

From Graves, C. (1963)

Clubs and Clubmen

By
MAJOR ARTHUR GRIFFITHS
Author of "The Rome Express," etc.

London: HUTCHINSON & CO.
Paternoster Row   1907

From Griffiths, A.G.F. (1907)

RECOLLECTIONS

By the Member of a Goose Club.

I PAID my shilling! paid it like a man,
   Though much my capital it did reduce;
But wildly my imagination ran
   Upon that luscious luxury, a goose!

Yes! I became the member of a Club—
   A Goose Club! Is it not a savoury thought?
But shall I win the prize? Ah! There's the rub!
   Or will experience be by failure bought?

I was a member of a Goose Club! Stay:
   Let me throw water on my fever'd brow.
My brain, at the remembrance of that day,
   Will be on fire. Ha! ha! 'tis burning now.

Yes! I subscrib'd my shilling! day by day
   I asked " Has fate destin'd that I should win?"
At night, as tossing on my bed I lay,
   I thought, " Will they give sage and onions in?"

At length, the Christmas feast was drawing near;
   The issue of my lot I soon should know:
There was a rumour, that of geese this year
   Immense would be the price, and small the show.

The long-expected evening came at last,
   The members of the Goose Club had all met,
Lots for the " foolish bird " were to be cast:
   I feel the heart-throb of that moment yet.

Our names were written out on paper strips,
   All of the Club distinctly taken down:
Jones, Tomkins, Spooner, Edwards, Burton, Phipps,
   Bendixen, Jackson, Oliphant, and Brown.

Ten were the members, while the goose was one—
   One only was the prize: the blanks were nine.
The lucky chance could be for one alone—
   I trembled as I hoped it would be mine.

As round the table anxiously we sat,
   The strips of paper were together cast,
And shaken up in a policeman's hat:
   My breath was thick, my pulse beat high and fast.

I seized a number, but I feared to look,
   I held it in my trembling fingers loose.
Had fate awarded me a goose to cook?
   Or had misfortune rudely cook'd my goose?

They caught the paper from my feeble grasp,
   As on my breast my throbbing temples sank;
I gave a side-long look—a groan—a gasp—
   A shriek—a gurgle—yes—it was a blank!

    *   *   *   *

Since then has many a " merry Christmas " pass'd,
   And I've received from fortune many a rub;
But that occasion was the first and last
   When I was goose enough to join a club.

Punch, 1853.

From Hammerton, J.A. – see p78

CLUB LAW.

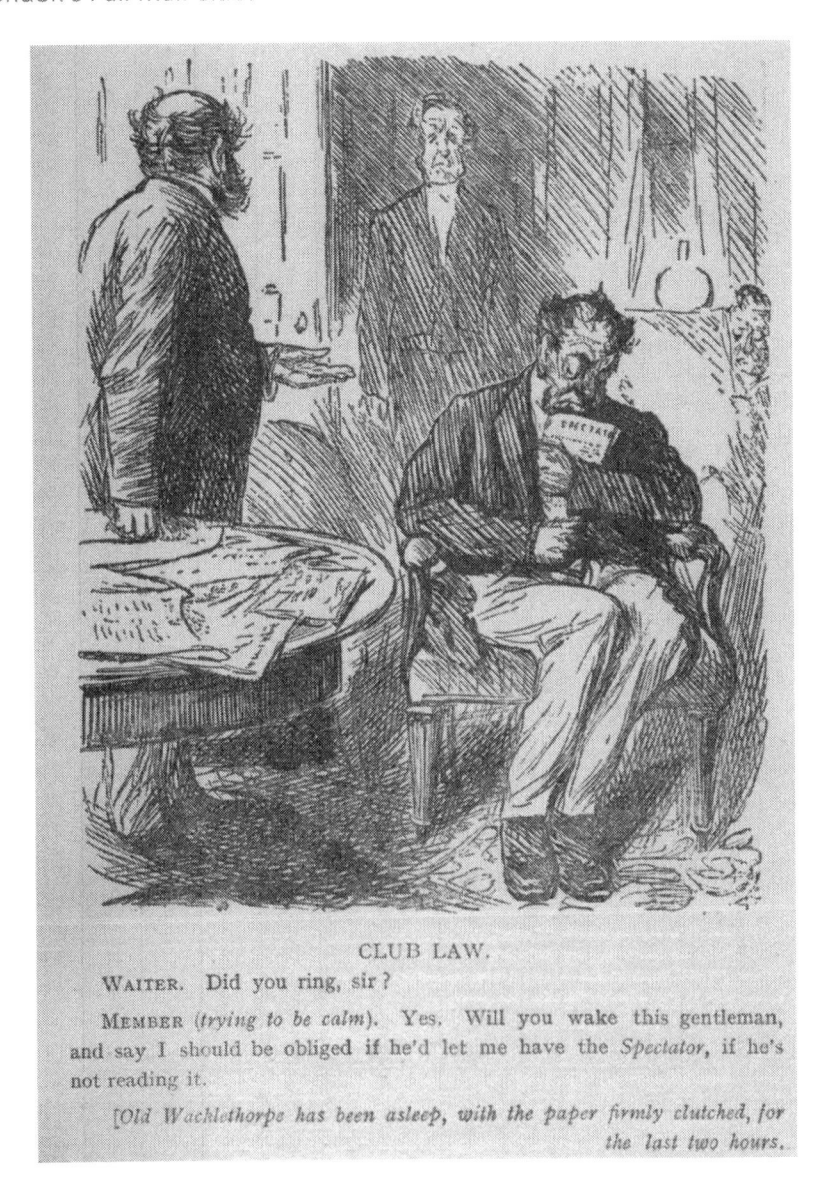

WAITER. Did you ring, sir?

MEMBER (*trying to be calm*). Yes. Will you wake this gentleman, and say I should be obliged if he'd let me have the *Spectator*, if he's not reading it.

[*Old Wachlethorpe has been asleep, with the paper firmly clutched, for the last two hours.*

From Hammerton

A Compendium of Images

TABLE-TURNING EXPERIMENT.

"There, old fella! hope you're satisfied it goes round now."
"Oh yesh! there's no mistake!"

From Hammerton

Club Attendant (to stout party, who is struggling into overcoat). "Allow me, sir."
Stout Party. "No, don't trouble! This is the only exercise I ever take!"

From Hammerton

A Compendium of Images

AT A LADIES' CLUB

Guest (who rather fancies himself as a fascinator). "But although you are all known as men-haters, aren't there now and again occasions when you find it *very* hard to live up to your reputation?"

From Hammerton

CLUB·LAND

London and Provincial

BY

JOSEPH HATTON

WITH FORTY-NINE ILLUSTRATIONS, INCLUDING SIXTEEN WHOLE-PAGE PLATES.

LONDON
J. S. VIRTUE & CO., Limited, 26, IVY LANE
1890

From Hatton, J. (1890).

A Compendium of Images

Arcade Room, Jockey Club.

From Hatton, J. (1890).

London's Pall Mall Clubs

Coffee Room, Jockey Club.

From Hatton, J. (1890).

A Compendium of Images

New Club, Edinburgh.

From Hatton, J. (1890).

203

New Club, Glasgow.

From Hatton, J. (1890).

Contents

Introduction	6	LANSDOWNE CLUB, THE	122
		MARYLEBONE CRICKET CLUB	128
ARMY & NAVY CLUB	16	NATIONAL LIBERAL CLUB, THE	134
ARTS CLUB, THE	20	NAVAL & MILITARY CLUB, THE	142
ATHENÆUM, THE	24	ORIENTAL CLUB, THE	150
BEEFSTEAK CLUB, THE	34	OXFORD & CAMBRIDGE CLUB	158
BOODLE'S	42	PRATT'S CLUB	166
BROOKS'S	48	RAF CLUB, THE	174
BUCK'S	58	REFORM CLUB, THE	182
CALEDONIAN CLUB, THE	64	SAVAGE CLUB, THE	190
CARLTON CLUB, THE	72	SAVILE CLUB, THE	196
CAVALRY & GUARDS CLUB	82	TRAVELLERS CLUB, THE	204
CITY CLUBS, THE	90	TURF CLUB, THE	216
EAST INDIA CLUB, THE	94	WHITE'S	224
FARMERS CLUB, THE	104		
GARRICK CLUB, THE	108	Acknowledgements	239
HURLINGHAM CLUB, THE	118	Select Bibliography	241

From Lejeune, A. (2012)

prevent the pancake sticking — the less you use the better. Test a ladle beforehand to work out how much batter in the ladle is necessary just to cover the bottom of the pan. Cook till pale brown on each side, turning it over with a palette-knife. As each one is cooked, take it out, drain it on paper, roll it up, sprinkle with sugar and keep it warm. Serve as soon as possible with pieces (not slices) of lemon and brown sugar (preferably Barbados Muscovado).

Sweet omelettes

Sweet omelettes are made in the same way as ordinary omelettes except that you substitute sugar for salt and pepper. You can put jam in the middle before you turn the omelette over on itself. If you want a rum omelette, heat some rum in a spoon or ladle and, when the omelette is on the plate, set fire to the rum and pour it, flaming, over the omelette.

Claret jelly

This comes from the New Club, Edinburgh.

'1 *bottle claret*   1 *teacup brandy*
juice and rind of a lemon   ½ *lb loaf sugar*
1 *teacup raspberry juice or*   1 *oz white leaf gelatine*
   red currant jelly

Boil all 10 minutes and put into a wet mould.
   Serve with vanilla cream sauce — ½ pint cream sweetened and flavoured with vanilla.'

Cerises Jubilee

This comes from Brooks's
   'Poach in a light syrup (½ pint water, 1 oz caster sugar) ½ lb of stoned black cherries for ten minutes. Remove the cherries to a serving dish. Reduce the syrup to half its quantity and add a measure of best Kirsch. Then pour this over the cherries and set alight. Can be served with vanilla ice-cream.'

From McDouall, R. (1974)

A Compendium of Images

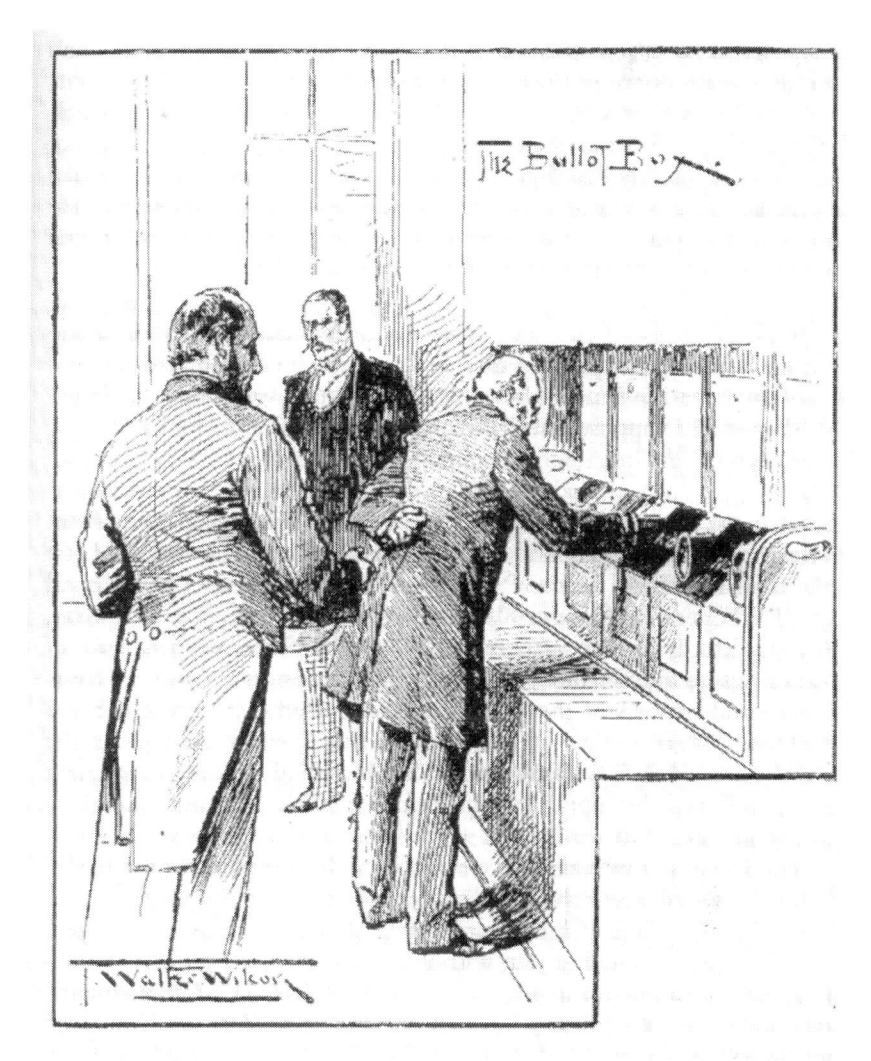

Figure 2.2. "The Athenaeum Club, Pall-Mall," *The Illustrated London News*, March 11, 1893, 308.

From Milne-Smith, A. (2011)

London's Pall Mall Clubs

Figure 3.2 "Expulsion of a Member from a Fashionable West-End Club," *Punch's Almanack*, 1914.

From Milne-Smith, A. (2011)

A Compendium of Images

AN OBJECT OF COMPASSION.

PITY AN UNFORTUNATE MAN, DETAINED IN LONDON BY UNINTERESTING CIRCUMSTANCES OVER WHICH HE HAS NO CONTROL, WHOSE FAMILY ARE ALL OUT OF TOWN, WHOSE ESTABLISHMENT IS REPRESENTED BY A CARETAKER, AND WHOSE CLUB IS CLOSED FOR ALTERATIONS AND REPAIRS.

Figure 5.3 "An Object of Compassion," *Punch*, August 23, 1890, 86.

From Milne-Smith, A. (2011)

XXIV.—CLUB HOUSES.

PRINCIPAL CLUBS IN LONDON:

Those marked with an asterisk (*) admit Strangers to dine in the Strangers' Room.

Name.	Number of Members limited to.	Entrance Fee.	Annual Subscription.	Where Situate.
		£ s.	£ s.	
*Army and Navy	1450	30 0	6 11	Pall-mall.
Arthur's	600	21 0	10 10	St. James's-st.
Athenæum	1200	26 5	6 6	Pall-mall.
Boodle's				28, St. James's-st.
Brooks's	575	9 9	11 11	St. James's-st.
Carlton	800 †	15 15	10 10	Pall-mall.
City of London		26 5	6 6	Old Broad-st., City
Cocoa Tree				St. James's-st.
*Conservative	1500	26 5	8 8	St. James's-st.
*Garrick	350	21 0	6 6	King-st., Covt-gn.
Guards	Officers of Hous. Troops only.			Pall-mall.
*Junior United Serv.	1500	30 0	6 0	Regent-street.
Oriental	800	21 0	8 0	Hanover-square.
*Oxford &Cambridge	1170 ‡	26 5	6 6	Pall-mall.
*Parthenon	700	21 0	7 7	Regent-street.
*Reform	1400 §	26 5	10 10	Pall-mall.
Travellers'	700	21 0	10 10	Pall-mall.
Union	1000	32 11	6 6	Trafalgar-square.
United Service	1500	30 0	6 0	Pall-mall.
*University Club	1000 ‖	26 5	6 0	Pall-mall.
White's	550			St. James's-st.
Whittington			2 2	Strand.
*Windham	600	27 6	8 0	St. James's-sq.

From the preceding table it will be seen that the twenty-six large clubs are nearly in one locality; nine being in Pall-mall, and four in St. James's-street, a district hence called Club-Land.

† Exclusive of Peers and Members of House of Commons.
‡ 585 from each University.
§ Exclusive of Honorary, Supernumerary, and Life Members.
‖ 500 of each University.

From Murray, J. (1860)

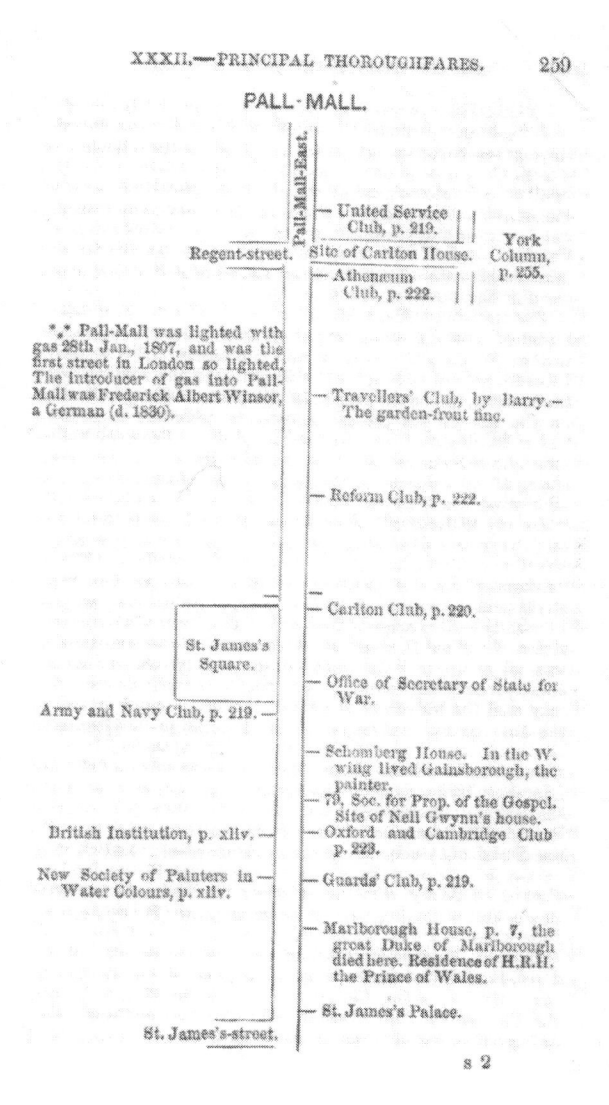

XXXII.—PRINCIPAL THOROUGHFARES.

PALL-MALL.

— United Service Club, p. 219.

Regent-street. Site of Carlton House.

York Column, p. 255.

— Athenæum Club, p. 222.

*** Pall-Mall was lighted with gas 28th Jan., 1807, and was the first street in London so lighted. The introducer of gas into Pall-Mall was Frederick Albert Winsor, a German (d. 1830).

— Travellers' Club, by Barry.—The garden-front fine.

— Reform Club, p. 222.

— Carlton Club, p. 220.

St. James's Square.

— Office of Secretary of State for War.

Army and Navy Club, p. 219.—

— Schomberg House. In the W. wing lived Gainsborough, the painter.
— 79, Soc. for Prop. of the Gospel. Site of Nell Gwynn's house.
— Oxford and Cambridge Club p. 223.

British Institution, p. xliv.—

New Society of Painters in Water Colours, p. xliv.—

— Guards' Club, p. 219.

— Marlborough House, p. 7, the great Duke of Marlborough died here. Residence of H.R.H. the Prince of Wales.

— St. James's Palace.

St. James's-street.

From Murray, J. (1860)

XXXII.—PRINCIPAL THOROUGHFARES.   265

ST. JAMES'S STREET.

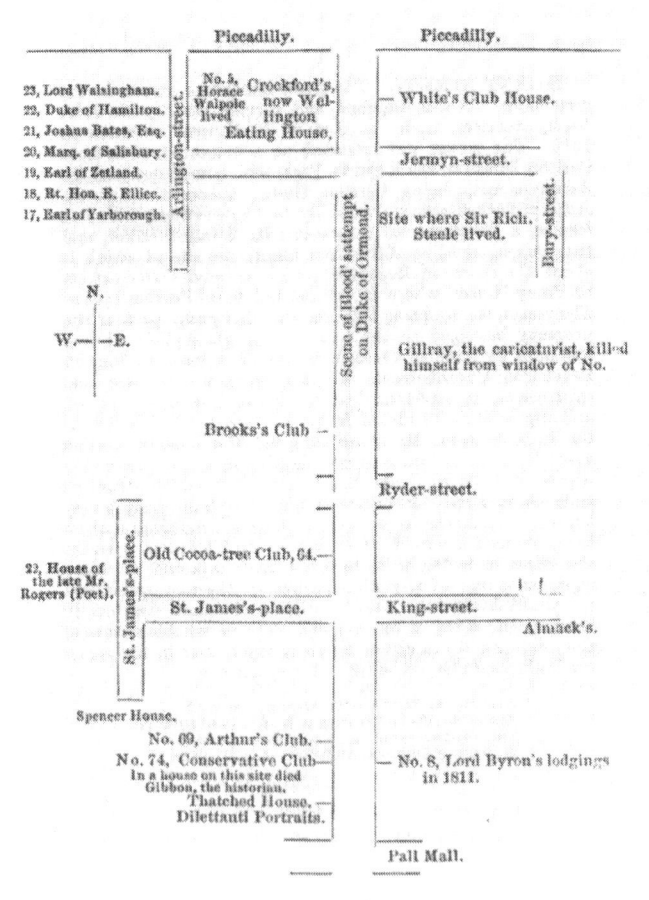

Piccadilly. | Piccadilly.

23, Lord Walsingham.
22, Duke of Hamilton.
21, Joshua Bates, Esq.
20, Marq. of Salisbury.
19, Earl of Zetland.
18, Rt. Hon. E. Ellice.
17, Earl of Yarborough.

No. 5. Crockford's, Horace Walpole lived — now Wellington Eating House.

— White's Club House.

Jermyn-street.

Site where Sir Rich. Steele lived.

Arlington-street.

Bury-street.

Scene of Blood's attempt on Duke of Ormond.

N.
W.—|—E.
S.

Gillray, the caricaturist, killed himself from window of No.

Brooks's Club —

Ryder-street.

22, House of the late Mr. Rogers (Poet).

Old Cocoa-tree Club, 64.—

St. James's-place.

St. James's-place.

King-street.

Almack's.

Spencer House.

No. 69, Arthur's Club. —
No. 74, Conservative Club—
In a house on this site died Gibbon, the historian.
Thatched House. —
Dilettanti Portraits.

— No. 8, Lord Byron's lodgings in 1811.

Pall Mall.

St. James's Palace.

From Murray, J. (1860)

LONDON CLUBS

THEIR HISTORY & TREASURES

By
RALPH NEVILL
AUTHOR OF "THE MERRY PAST," "LIGHT COME, LIGHT GO," ETC.

LONDON: CHATTO & WINDUS
MDCCCCXI

From Nevill, R. (1911)

From O'Connor, A. (1976)

A Compendium of Images

From Thackeray, W.M. (1848)

London's Pall Mall Clubs

From Thackeray, W.M. (1848)

A Compendium of Images

From Thackeray, W.M. (1848)

London's Pall Mall Clubs

From Thackeray, W.M. (1848)

A Compendium of Images

Sir Reginald Blomfield by Ginsbury, c. 1906

From Thole, J. (1992)

219

THE ROXBURGHE CLUB DINNERS.

The bill of fare was as follows:—

FIRST COURSE.

Turtle.*

Turtle Cutlets.   Turtle Fin.

Turbot.

Boiled Chickens.   Ham.
Sauté of Haddock.   Chartreuse.
Turtle.   *Frame.*   Turtle.
Tendrons of Lamb.   Fillets of Whitings.

Tongue.   R. Chickens.
Turtle Fin.   John Dory.   Fricandeau of Turtle.

Turtle.*

†‡† Cold Roast Beef on Side Tables.
* These Tureens were removed for two dishes of White Bait.

SECOND COURSE.

Venison (2 Haunches).

THIRD COURSE.

Larded Poults.

Tart.   Cheese Cakes.

Artichoke bottoms.

Jelly.   Prawns.

B. Quails.   R. Leveret.

Salade Italienne.   Crême Italienne.

Peas.

Cabinet Pudding.   Tourt.

R. Goose.

The bill, as a specimen of the advantages of separate charges, as well as on other accounts, may be worth preserving:—

From Timbs, J. (1866)

CLUB LIFE OF LONDON

WITH

ANECDOTES OF THE CLUBS, COFFEE-HOUSES AND TAVERNS OF THE METROPOLIS

DURING THE 17TH, 18TH, AND 19TH CENTURIES.

BY JOHN TIMBS, F.S.A.

Beef-steak Society's Emblem.

IN TWO VOLUMES.—VOL. I.

LONDON:
RICHARD BENTLEY, NEW BURLINGTON STREET,
Publisher in Ordinary to Her Majesty.
1866.

From Timbs, J. (1866)

THE SECOND PART

OF THE

LONDON CLUBS

CONTAINING.

THE NO NOSE CLUB   THL MOLLIES CLUB
THE BEAUS CLUB.   THE QUACKS CLUB.

BY THE AUTHOR OF THE LONDON SPY.

LONDON, PRINTED BY J. DUTTON, NEAR FLEET STREET.
Also the First Part.

From Ward, E. (1709)

A Compendium of Images

From Wintle, A.D. (1961)

London's Pall Mall Clubs

THE AUTHOR

COLONEL A. D. WINTLE, M.C., F.R.S.L., was born at Marioupol in Russia in 1897 of English parentage. A veteran of both World Wars, his published works are numerous, his career long and colourful, including in recent years the successful conduct of his own case in a series of legal actions, culminating in his triumphant, unanimous win in the House of Lords. Colonel Wintle lives at Wrotham in Kent.

photo by Pearl Freeman

From Wintle, A.D. (1961)

A Compendium of Images

His hair had grown so long it made The Club look untidy
(*Page 40*)

From Wintle, A.D. (1961)

225

A brief note on the two sister volumes

A brief note on the two sister volumes so far published in the London series:
The Livery Companies and the Inns volumes are in matching hardback bindings.

London's Livery Companies (with a Foreword by the 680th Lord Mayor of London)

About 40,000 people belong to over 100 City Companies within the Square Mile of the City of London. These institutions are commonly referred to as the Livery Companies and the earliest dates back to 1155. This book is the only comprehensive study of these Livery Companies for over seventy years, and for the first time shows just how extensive is their range of charitable activity as well as explaining that: they are not connected to Freemasonry; some are very wealthy indeed; new ones are quite frequently added (say, the Tax Advisers in 2005) while over the centuries others have withered away as their trades or 'misteries' have disappeared (for instance, the

Bowyers or the Loriners); their medieval role was part economic and part social; the London Liverymen played a crucial part in 1641/1642 as Parliament forced the King to flee from his capital; the Livery Companies came close to being 'reformed' out of (a supposedly corrupt) existence in the 1880s; great nineteenth-century authors such as Dickens, Thackeray, and Trollope had much to say about the Companies; similar organisations still function in Bristol and Sheffield; they are oligarchic chartered corporations regulated by the City of London Corporation, but they are not charities even if they control and fund related charities; the Liverymen elect the Lord Mayor of the Corporation; some own splendid historic Halls stuffed with treasures; and so on… But are these City Companies fit-for-purpose after nearly 900 years and at the start of a new century - or are they well past their institutional sell-by-date? Quaint and quirky, and eccentrically English: to be cherished or condemned? And why are they labelled 'The Worshipful Company of…'?

London's Inns of Court (with a Foreword by Lord Justice Rix, Court of Appeal)

This volume is the first broad study of the four Inns (each 'The Honourable Company of …') since the 1930s, of what has been called 'the legal university' as 'the third university' for many centuries when only Oxford and Cambridge existed south of Hadrian's Wall. It explores: their history dating back to the middle of the fourteenth-century; their rather odd legal status as unincorporated associations; their accounts and assets; their role in training barristers; their provision of Chambers for collectives of such legal creatures; the purpose of the compulsory dinners in their splendid Halls for the trainee-barristers; the disappearance of the Inns of Chancery and the redeployment of their assets; and how the Inns and 'the Bar' are portrayed by such as Shakespeare, Dickens,

Thackeray, and Trollope. Still 'a good thing' after almost 700 years at the dawn of the new century and given the Legal Services Act 2007 that seeks to liberalise and deregulate the legal profession? Or an expensive anachronism, little more than a tourist attraction in terms of the functioning of the legal system in a digital age?

Printed in Great Britain
by Amazon